In lyrical prose that her readers to places they might never go unaccompanied. As she searches alone for self-fulfillment and love in the British Columbia bush or a Ganges River ashram; in a Roman *piazza* or a Kashmiri houseboat, her readers learn about themselves too.

– Lynne Bowen, author of *Boss Whistle*

Engaging, insightful, and delightfully entertaining. *Every Day We Disappear* takes memoir to a whole new level.

–Andreas Schroeder, author of *Dust Ship Glory*

The writing is so unaffectedly deft and alert that it would be tempting to race through this chronicle at one sitting, as if it were a deck of soothsayer's cards laid out one after another. That would be a mistake, for each card has a revelation that lingers like a poem. Angela Long travels the world and the heart's unruly byways disguised as an innocent waif, with a wickedly kind eye and ear for place, culture, and character. The innocence is real, though – vulnerable, heartsick, too easily bruised by encounters with poverty, unfairness and simple endurance, and yet at the same time it is completely and wonderingly mischievous.

–Sean Virgo, author of *The Shadow Mother*

every day we disappear

BY ANGELA LONG

radiant press

To John and Coleen!
My favourite
westcoast loggers
ever.
Love
K.L.

Editor: dee Hobsbawn-Smith
Cover Photo: Angela Long
Book and cover design: Tania Wolk, Third Wolf Studio
Printed and bound in Canada at Friesens, Altona, MB

The publisher gratefully acknowledges the support of Creative Saskatchewan and Saskatchewan
Arts Board. The author would like to thank the Canada Council for the Arts for their assistance
and support of this book.

Library and Archives Canada Cataloguing in Publication:
Long, Angela, 1971-, author
Every day We disappear / Angela Long.

Issued in print and electronic formats.
ISBN 978-1-77518-393-8 (softcover).--ISBN 978-1-77518-394-5 (PDF)

1. Long, Angela, 1971- --Travel. 2. Authors, Canadian (English)--
Travel. 3. Voyages and travels. I. Title.

PS8623.O525Z46 2018 C811'.6 C2018-904749-6
C2018-904750-X

Radiant Press
Box 33128 Cathedral PO
Regina, SK S4T 7X2
info@radiantpress.ca
www.radiantpress.ca

radiant press

AUTHOR'S NOTE

The stories in this book reflect the author's recollection of events. Some names and identifying characteristics have been changed to protect the privacy of those depicted.

table of contents

introduction

THE TRAIN TO ANYWHERE

I STAND IN AMSTERDAM Central Station, staring up at the departure board. I am alone for the first time ever, it seems, in possession of two thousand dollars' worth of American Express travellers cheques, a large sum of money for an eighteen-year-old in 1989.

I've earned it by deep-frying doughnuts from midnight until eight in the morning, six days a week, in a bakery on a Canadian military base in West Germany. My big brother Todd is serving as a master corporal in the Canadian military, and I've been living with him and his wife in a town called Oberschopfheim since I graduated from high school two months earlier in Canada. Just a few days ago, we rented a Mercedes and drove to Amsterdam for a little brother-sister bonding in the hash dens and tulip fields.

Todd gives me a quick hug beside the ticket counter. His buddies are probably waiting for him at the Bulldog. I'm supposed to catch the 2:34 p.m. to Cherbourg, and then ferry across to England. But, suddenly, as I watch my brother's lanky frame disappear through the glass doors, I don't want to go to England anymore.

I walk over to the departures board, and scan it for the first train that's scheduled to depart. A train to Anywhere. It leaves in five minutes. I buy a ticket. I have no guidebook, hotel reservations, or any idea how long it takes to get to Anywhere. But, none of that seems important. I feel alive, alive in every nerve-tingly sense of the word.

I hurry toward the platform, lurching beneath the monstrous backpack flopping behind me like a dying fish. I smile at my fellow passengers on their way to Anywhere, convinced we're part of some magical master plot together.

When the train pulls out of the station, I feel my pulse quicken. I'm so excited I can barely hear the conductor ask for my ticket. "All the way?" he asks in English. "Are you going all the way to –" I no more want to hear him utter that name than deep-fry another doughnut. I've fallen in love with something, but, as is often the case, I don't know with what.

Twenty years later, I know. I had fallen in love with a moment of unfurling. A moment when an industrial parkland on the outskirts of Amsterdam became the most beautiful sight I'd ever seen. A moment I knew existed but had never witnessed – like the opening of a flower. I had been in love with being a flower – exposed, vulnerable, flaunting the colours of my naïveté. I must have known it was imperative for my survival to be that way. Without unfurling my petals, how could I have hoped to photosynthesize, to pollinate?

These days when I Google location, transportation, and accommodation options well in advance of an upcoming holiday, I wonder when those petals began to wilt. I analyze costs, schedules, and the potential positive and negative aspects of each choice as though I'm coordinating a voyage to Saturn. Why not just let go? Why, when I have so many more resources and travel smarts than my eighteen-year-old self, am I so much more afraid?

It has become too easy to substitute comfort and security for living. I throw away my calculations and look for my old backpack instead. It's time to catch that train to Anywhere.

part one

GO BIG OR GO HOME

"DO YOU HAVE FIRE?" the stranger asked. He held up a pack of tobacco. Drum.

I laughed. "Do you mean a light?"

I could tell he was French Canadian. A blue-eyed, long-lashed, dark-haired mix of Old France and New World. Later, he'd tell me he was related to Jack Kerouac, and I won't be surprised.

We were tree planters, working in the "bush" of northern British Columbia. We lived in tents, ate in tents, and shat behind a tarp in a tent. All day long, we bent, dug, and slid trees into the ground as fast and as frequently as our bodies and minds would allow. For some reason this environment bred romance as quickly as mosquitoes.

I left the screen door zipped tightly shut as I rustled around my tent to find a box of wooden emergency matches. I felt how I often had when I was twenty-one, like a boring Caucasian middle-class girl from Oshawa – a suburb in southern Ontario bookended by General Motors and Darlington Nuclear Generating Station – who didn't do things like smoke. It was inevitable I'd fall in love with him from the first drag he took of his hand-rolled cigarette. He cocked his chin towards the sky, funneling smoke through his lips. The crickets began their chorus. The sky deepened to a perfect hue of sapphire. And in this dusky light, he looked as wild and beautiful as any creature I'd hoped to encounter in the British Columbian bush.

I'd come to the West to re-invent myself. Since arriving, I'd met people with VW vans and shampoo made from chamomile flowers. I wore Birkenstocks now, and colourful bandanas. The new me could have unzipped her tent door all the way. She could have stripped off her layers of fleece and wool. She could have said – Yes, I have fire. You just lit it.

Instead I crouched behind the screen, conscious of the pink long underwear my mother had given me. As the stranger took another drag, there was a chance to say something witty with a dash of sexiness. But Oshawa oozed from me like bug repellant.

"I'm Michel," the stranger said as he turned to go.

"Michel," I repeated, careful to get the accent right.

It took a week before we spoke again. A week of me trying to look nonchalant when we lined up for dinner or sat around the campfire at night to keep warm.

"Comment ça va?" I asked as he sat down beside me, the only vacant place left in the dining tent. I thought I knew how to speak French, after studying it all the way to the end of high school.

"You speak French?" he said, and began talking at an alarming pace. I smiled and nodded until it was evident I had no idea what he was talking about.

~

AS THE SEASON PROGRESSED, it became increasingly difficult to look attractive. The weather wasn't on my side. It rained, hailed, snowed. The only mirror I had access to was the side mirror of the pick-up truck (otherwise known as the crummy). I examined my reflection when no one was around. What I saw alarmed me. Dirt blocked every pore. My bandana had slid back, revealing the secret bobby pins I'd inserted to control my frizzy locks.

The other women in the camp, women who'd grown up in this province and looked as lush as their surroundings, were confident in Michel's presence. They all wore the same types of clothing – colourful, ethnic-looking stuff – faded just enough to show they'd always dressed this way. Their hair was long and disheveled. They knew how to roll joints. They looked at Michel exactly like the predators they were.

You see, Michel was the camp's highballer – a title given to the person who consistently planted the most trees. It was easy to know who this was. At the end of every shift, when everyone piled back into the crummy, dirty and sweaty and exhausted, the foreman got out his dog-eared notepad and did roll call.

"Bradfield?"

"1050."

"Mooney?"

"1375."

The highballer usually doubled everyone else's numbers. Double the numbers, double the money.

It would be at least ten years, just into the new millennium, before tree planting was elevated to "silviculture" and online resources like

"A Tree Planter's Guide to Reducing Musculoskeletal Injuries" existed. Our foreman's motto was "Go big or go home." Those were the days of a non-unionized, non-online community, non-WorkSafe free-for-all. You could still dip tree seedlings in pesticides, then eat a sandwich. It would be a while before people planted trees with the goal of saving the environment. Things were simpler back then. You planted to make money. And whoever made the most money was the highballer.

Highballers were the gods of the camp. They strutted through the cook tent at the end of the day attended to by their minions. They drank scotch with the foremen in heated trailers. The cooks offered them prime cuts of meat. We needed something to worship in those godforsaken outposts of clear-cut, swamp, and slash. The highballers were our heroes.

I was the camp lowballer. I wore matching outfits acquired at Mark's Work Warehouse in Oshawa. Clothing I had thought would suit this type of work – cotton work pants and matching shirts – while everyone else wore long underwear with boxer shorts over top, and either ratty grey Stanfields or ironic T-shirts ("Ringette Rules!") curated from thrift stores on days off.

It would have been natural for Michel to couple with the highballer goddess. Every morning she jumped out of the crummy before I'd even pulled on my boots. She streaked across her allotted chunk of clear-cut, auburn hair streaming behind her like the tail of a comet. I watched, dreading the moment I'd clip on my bags filled with tree seedlings and dig the first hole. I dreaded the hole after hole, the tree after tree, the desolation I'd feel later, when I'd lose sight of the rest of the crew, and stand alone in the clear-cut amongst the stumps and roots.

Sometimes the land had been burned — napalmed — black and desolate as far as the eye could see. Once while pulling on my cork boots at the edge of a 300-square kilometre clear-cut in the Bowron River Valley, my foreman looked from the boxes of tree seedlings to the sweep of land void of any sign of life. "They say you can see this from outer space," he said.

In later years, planting on Vancouver Island, sometimes I'd stand on the edge of the remaining old growth, peering in to see what had once existed: majestic cedars and spruce, green carpets of fern and moss. At these times, I'd lay down my shovel. Sometimes, I'd weep.

But something would always make me pick up my shovel again, and plant. I'd plant in the sun, rain, sleet, snow. I'd plant with mosquitoes buzzing from all sides, biting anything exposed. It was lonely work. Repetitive work. But it made me lean; after a few weeks, I was a finely honed machine of pure muscle. There was nothing I wouldn't be able to do after tree planting. No job would be too strenuous or too dirty.

At the end of the first shift we celebrated with a bonfire. The foreman dragged deadfall from the forest and threw it whole onto the blaze. "Go big or go home!" he yelled. We cheered. Clouds of sparks exploded in the sky. Suddenly, I noticed Michel watching me from across the fire. He walked in my direction, can of Lucky in hand, and sat down. I stared into the blue heart of a flame.

"Why are you here?" he asked and lit up a cigarette.

"I'm trying to save money for university," I said, taking a sip of Bacardi Breezer.

Michel laughed. "Why do you want to go to university?"

No one had ever asked me that before. University was just something you did, like get married and have children.

Michel took one of my hands and flipped it over. My palms were cracked and raw from pesticides and dirt. Our foreman forbade the use of gloves, thinking they slowed us down. But Michel didn't obey that rule. His hands felt as smooth as silk.

"You should wear gloves, you know."

I nodded, too nervous to speak.

"Do you want to hitch to Mexico with me when this is over?"

"Yes." I didn't hesitate. I didn't care that I'd been just accepted into the University of Victoria's Creative Writing Program. I didn't care that Michel was drunk and stoned and would forget about all of this in the morning. But he didn't forget.

~

"Make sure you look them in the eye," Michel said. He unclipped his backpack, hid it in the ditch, and told me to do the same. "They trust you if you look them in the eye. But if they don't look back, and they stop, don't get in the car. Never trust anyone who won't look you in the eye."

A car approached from the base of the hill. We stood on top of the only hill I could see in this corner of B.C., somewhere north of Fort Nelson, and just south of the Yukon. Our exact location, like many planting camps in this part of the world, was a mere coordinate marked by surveyors on a cutblock map. But we knew we were thousands of miles from the Mexican border. Muskeg dotted with islands of black spruce stretched in all directions. Just this morning we'd been part of that landscape, sweating in a tent scorched by the July sun.

The last few weeks of the summer contract hadn't been much fun. First the giardia outbreak caused by water from a contaminated stream the foreman decided to pump into camp, then the replants ordered by the "checker from hell" who measured every millimetre of space between the seedlings we'd spent days planting, then the hours long journey by rolligon (a tank-like vehicle nicknamed the "Slimer") into a clear-cut where a swamp stank like a septic tank and it was light nearly twenty-four hours a day. All this for ten cents, or less, per tree. First the highballers went on strike. Then, one by one, they quit.

"That's enough," Michel had said. "Let's get out of here." By that point, Michel had moved into my more spacious tent. It didn't take much for me to agree to quit too. I would have left in April if I hadn't been so in love, enduring the daily misery for the excitement that awaited every night in the glow of our red tent.

I unclipped my pack and set it beside his.

"Okay, Ang. Stick out your thumb so they can see you well in advance."

I'd never hitched before. Where I came from, hitching was reserved for vagabonds, prostitutes, and drug addicts, or so my mother had told me every time we passed one by. Michel had hitched across Canada twice, from Mexico to Montréal once. I stood with my arm slack by my side. I was shy. Ashamed.

"Now, Ang, now," Michel encouraged.

For a second, I caught the driver's eye, then looked away. The car drove past, the only car we'd seen for the past hour.

"That's okay, we're in no hurry," he said and kissed me.

It felt like hours before I was given another chance. This time I looked into the driver's eyes as though we'd always known one another and planned to meet here, on the side of this road, when the sun began to set and the mosquitoes began to bite. I raised my arm. Stuck my thumb high into the air as though I was from the big wide world instead of little ol' Oshawa.

"You remind me of my daughter," the elderly gentleman said as I climbed into the cab of his truck and Michel threw our packs in the back. "Couldn't leave my daughter standing out there, could I?"

THE AMERICAN

THE AMERICAN SHOOK A COCONUT beside his ear: "Gotta make sure you can hear the juice swish." He wore sandals with rubber-tire soles, just like the locals. He spoke Spanish with a southern drawl and called the vendors by name.

Soon Michel would buy the exact same sandals. For now he looked into the blue eyes of this man with the long white hair and matching beard like he'd found a long-lost relative. We'd spent too long in the hippy haven of Mexico's Zipolite for Michel's liking. After two months of making love in the Pacific, on the beach, in our cabana, on a hammock (challenging), activities which caused an embarrassing vaginal infection the local doctor attributed to sand, we'd decided to take what little money we had left and head to an even cheaper country, one that I'd never even heard of: Guatemala. It was time for some serious travel, Michel had said.

Salvador, the coconut seller, shaved off a thin swath of husk, like a barber shaving a balloon. Swift stroke of machete, quick poke of straw through meat.

"First jugo de cocó?" the American asked.

Sì. My first coconut juice. My first everything. First time south of Florida, first time speaking Spanish, first time seeing children beg in a restaurant, and a body lying on the road, spooning the curve. "Bus accident," they'd told me.

I sipped. Tepid. Sweet. A piece of flesh caught in the straw.

"Bus accident?" The American smiled. His name was David. He'd been in Guatemala a while. "I sought asylum here from the insanity of the U. S. of A. in 1987," he told us over glasses of freshly pressed sugar cane juice at the thatched hut he shared with Elena, his Mayan wife.

David took Michel and me under his wing. He ran Cocina Para Los Niños – a soup kitchen in touristy Panajachel he'd started for street kids from villages surrounding Lake Atitlán who'd been orphaned during the civil war.

"Civil war?" I asked.

"It's best not to talk about it," he warned. "Especially here." He pointed to the vendors watching us from the perimeter of the market. "You never know who could be listening."

Instead the three of us talked at Cocina Para Los Niños, chopping carrots for the soup, thinning corn syrup with water to drizzle on the pancakes.

David claimed to have done everything from owning a chain of Italian restaurants to becoming a millionaire (twice) to living on a commune in Arizona to running a furniture business.

"Luckily I saw the light one day," he said, "walking downtown New York. A stranger comes up to me. She says, 'Go to India and meet Sai Baba' then hands me an envelope stuffed with cash."

"Sai Baba?" I asked.

"Oh, honey. We gotta lot of catching up to do."

Luckily, David loved to talk. It was David who told us to read Diet for a New America and Noam Chomsky. He taught us how to make furniture from avocado wood, and the perfect guacamole. He was a self-taught expert in orchid cultivation, wheat grass, Mayan weaving. He called Michel "brother" and I became "sister." He found us a tin-roofed shack near Lake Atitlán beside a mango tree.

And I dreamed of Sai Baba. I saw the orange robes and black Afro of the photo David had taped to the wall of his hut. I heard music.

"Is this the music you heard?" David asked, and played a cassette. It was. "Promise me you'll go to India someday, sister."

THE ENGLISH SCHOOL

1. Greetings

IT'S NINE O'CLOCK IN THE MORNING. The sun inches above the lime trees of Panajachel. Beyond the gates of the English school, the highlands turn a brighter shade of green.

"Hello. My name is Angela. What's your name?"

I look towards the man with the threadbare shirt so perfectly pressed. He says, "Your name is Miguel."

Heat rises from the underbelly of the dirt floor. Sweat rings bloom on my blouse. "My name is Angela. I am from Canada. Where are you from?"

I look towards the woman sitting by the window, the woman with glossy hair so perfectly braided. One front tooth black with rot. She says, "My name is Canada."

I turn to the blackboard, pick up a piece of chalk. Even this is hot, difficult to grasp. I write: Hello, my name is Angela. I turn and begin again.

2. The Interrogative

THE AVOCADOES DROP LIKE BOMBS on the tin roof. "Repeat after me," I say. "When, when did the killings start?" An avocado drops like a bomb. Mateo ducks beneath the desk for cover. They are large, as big as grapefruits. A squeeze of lemon, a sprinkle of salt. Quickly, I crawl onto the roof. The ants are already there. "Repeat after me," I say. "Who, who are the soldiers in the trucks?"

Their flesh is a creamy jade. Green butter. There is no time to smear it on bread or crackers, you have to scoop it out, quickly, with your fingers, before the next bomb falls.

3. The Time

"WHAT TIME IS IT?" I ask, pointing to my watch, noticing the students' bare wrists.

Miguel examines shadows cast by the orange trees. "Almost twelve o'clock," he says.

"Yes, noon," I say. "It's almost noon."

It's almost time for class to end, for Miguel to pick up his machete, for Maria to go home to her tin-roofed shack, for Rigo to pull closed the shutters of his shop.

"What time is it?" I ask, drawing a clock on the blackboard, two hands meeting at the top, a crescent of moon, a smattering of stars.

"Twelve o'clock," says Maria.

"Yes, midnight," I say.

Midnight, almost time for the cantina to close, for the music to stop and the men to stagger along dirt paths and sleep where they fall. "Midnight," I say, thinking of those men, how they are still there at quarter past, at half past, at every hour upon the hour, their calloused feet, weather-worn skin, stench of fermented maize, how they curl into the Earth like unwanted fetuses.

A FAMILIAR FACE

It arrived during Montréal's cold snap of 1994. A yellow envelope. A franked U.S. stamp. If I'd recognized the return address, maybe I would have waited for a different moment to open it. A solitary moment in a quiet place. On this day, I opened it how I usually opened letters back then, with a careless rip en route from the front door to the living room where our two roommates, the film students, sat watching movies all day.

I can't remember what they were watching, or whether they noticed the expression on my face. I remember going into my frigid bedroom and sitting on the futon. I put the letter down and looked out the window at the icy-white sky for a long, long time.

At some point I picked up the letter again. "Call me collect," she wrote. There was a phone number. A name signed with a flourish: Patricia Gallagher. My mother. The mother who'd given me up for adoption when I was a baby. Gallagher. I tried the name on. I said it aloud. I stared out the window, watching the sky turn a pale rose.

When Michel came home from work, I could barely speak I was so overwhelmed. "She wrote," was all I could say. But he knew who I was talking about. I showed him the letter.

"Call her," he said.

I'd waited for this moment for so many years that, as I picked up the phone and stared at the numbers on the console, I couldn't bring myself to press them. Every number seemed to represent a different year of my life. Years when she hadn't been there.

I held the receiver away from me. How could a person who used such bright yellow stationery abandon her baby? Had she been living it up in Arizona all this time? I put the phone down. Slammed it a little.

Michel came back into the room. He gave me a long, hard look. "Call her, Angie," he said. "You don't know her story."

Maybe it was too late in Arizona to call, I reasoned. What was the time zone there anyway? Maybe it was best to wait until Sunday. Sunday afternoon when our roommates would be at Cinéma du Parc. Michel kept looking at me. I took a deep breath and dialled.

~

EVEN THOUGH MY ADOPTIVE parents had done their best to make me feel like part of the family, I, a pale-skinned, blonde-headed wisp of a girl, might as well have been beamed down from Mars as picked up from a hospital ward in Ottawa. They and their two naturally-born sons were a merry, olive-toned, large-boned bunch. Naturally, whenever the family appeared in public, strangers had wondered where I'd come from. "Where'd she get that blonde hair?" they'd ask. "Oh, her father was blond when he was young," answered my mother, who had never lied otherwise.

This little white lie had never failed to make me wonder: What were they hiding? I began to feel like adoption was a dirty word. It was our little secret. My parents must have told me before I could talk; maybe they'd sung it to me in a lullaby. But they hadn't told me when I was old enough to know what it meant.

I'd learned what it meant in the schoolyard. It was something no one wanted to be. "You're adopted!" was a popular insult of the time. Being adopted was a fact I'd hidden on family tree day, drawing branches leading from one fictitious name to another. It had never occurred to me to learn of my adopted family's ancestry. I must have figured it was better to lie than pretend to be someone I wasn't.

And who was I? I'd convinced myself the answer to this question lay in the discovery of my birth mother. I looked for her, at the grocery store, the library, the mall.

Eventually I'd been forced to acknowledge I already had a mother, someone who taught me things like how to draw leaves and make grilled cheese sandwiches. At the time I didn't recognize my childhood as whimsical. I was too busy exploring meadows and putting on puppet plays. I'd had little reason to feel sorry for myself. But still, I'd been curious.

I was twenty-two before I did anything to satisfy this curiosity. My efforts were sparked by an encounter with a woman I met in French class during a brief stint at Ottawa's Carleton University when I was twenty. She too was adopted. She'd gone through the process of finding her birth mother, and discovered she was the child of a rape. "But it didn't matter," she told me. She told me about instant bonds, about the pieces of her life falling into place.

I couldn't wait for the pieces of my life to fall into place. Since Guatemala, I'd ridden the bus from Panajachel to Vancouver. Collected welfare. Been employed as a dishwasher, tree planter, waitress, cook, telemarketer. I'd stopped shaving my legs. I'd tried to sell woven bracelets, painted flower pots, papier mâché mirror frames. Michel had split up with me while canoeing down the Rio Petén on Guatemala's east coast, while hiking from village to village around Lake Atitlán, while cycling to Victoria, B.C.'s Gordon Head. He'd begged my forgiveness in hotel rooms, dirt-floored huts, VW vans, Montréal pubs.

After our latest reconciliation and my move into Michel's and the film students' rue Berri apartment, I called the Ontario Adoption Registry. They told me forms would arrive soon. They asked: "Do you know if your name has been changed? Do you know your birth-registration number?"

Next, I called my adoptive mother. "What?" she asked, surprised. "Please don't take this personally," I said. Silence. "I just want to know my medical history and that kind of stuff," I lied.

I lied because I didn't want to hurt her feelings. How could I have told her I wanted to see someone who looked like me? How could I have told her I wanted an instant bond?

I prepared for the wait. I'd been advised the hiatus could last anywhere from months to years to infinity. I had to wait because a reunion could take place only if my birth mother also consented to be contacted. Someday, they told me, if all the pieces were found, a letter might arrive. Or a phone call.

~

THE PHONE RANG. Someone picked it up after the first ring, as though they'd been waiting. At first, I thought I was hearing my voice echo. "Hello?" I repeated. There was no sense asking the woman on the end of the other line if she was Patricia Gallagher.

"Hello?" she asked with the same soft voice I've been told I possess, a voice well suited for phone sex or hypnotherapy.

"Angela?" she asked, just to make sure.

"Just call me Angie," I said.

"Just call me Pat," she said. We laughed.

When Michel left the room, I couldn't hold in my emotion any longer. Tears that had waited far too long to fall blurred my view of the Montréal sky. Suddenly it didn't make sense to try to make conversation.

But Pat sat there with me, three time zones away. She sat wherever she was sitting, staring out at whatever she stared out at – A cactus? A canyon? She wasn't going anywhere this time.

After a while I sensed the temperature had dropped outside. There was a stillness out there, of a cold where snow doesn't crunch beneath footsteps, where branches seize, where people barricade themselves indoors ferreting out warmth. I stopped crying.

"Maybe it's better if we meet in person," Pat said.

~

THE AIRPORT IN ALBUQUERQUE was a four-hour drive from Pat's home in Arizona's White Mountains. She had told me she'd meet me at the airport with her husband and son. There was a husband. A son. I slung on my backpack and began to walk in the direction of the arrivals lounge until my nerves got the better of me.

The entire journey had been a battle against nerves. Bouts of diarrhea and nausea. Sweaty palms and nonsensical conversation with fellow passengers and airline staff. At every checkpoint I'd debated turning back and calling it a day.

On the way to the arrivals lounge, I stopped in front of a Mexican restaurant. It was happy hour. I decided to delay reality a little longer. I ordered a margarita and ate tortilla chips with salsa. Spicy salsa with fresh cilantro. I convinced myself I was on a holiday. Just a simple holiday. I wasn't here to meet the woman who was my birth mother and her twelve-year old son who, I realized with a start, was actually my half brother.

I knew they were waiting out there, but I couldn't move from the rattan seat. I admired the palm trees jutting towards the airport skylights and the southern accent of my waiter.

And then I saw her, rounding the bend near the magazine stand. She was with a skinny boy who looked even more nervous than me. She looked like a mid-forties version of me. Long, grey hair. Slightly frizzy.

No make-up. Slight frame. She was wearing tight jeans and a sweatshirt printed with a wolf padding along the top of a mesa.

It was disconcerting to watch my older self scan the corridor leading to the baggage carousels with such a look of worry. The boy looked in the direction of the restaurant. Quickly, I settled the bill.

The moment I stepped out into the main corridor, my birth mother zoned in on me. She looked at me like you'd look at a glass of water after a long day in the desert. That look scared me so much that I focused on the skylights again. The sky was darkening. Then I fiddled industriously with the straps on my backpack until she got so close I was forced to acknowledge her presence.

"Angie?" she asked, as if I could be anyone else. She had a similar version of my backpack slung over the same shoulder. I managed a nod. "I thought you'd decided not to come," she said.

It was time for the awkward moment then. The moment I'd spent years dreaming about. I'd imagined many things: running into one another's arms; a frenzied embrace; copious tears. I hadn't imagined a wide-eyed boy sizing me up, or the smell of tequila on my breath.

The right moment wasn't here in the Albuquerque airport with Texans in cowboy hats looking on from the restaurant. The right time wasn't accompanied by announcements for departures to Salt Lake City.

We embraced. Quickly. I turned to her son, my brother, and we smiled at one another. "This is Lee," Pat said.

He gazed at me like you'd only gaze at your long-lost-big-sister fresh from the North. "Hi," he said quickly and looked away, towards the magazine stand. The husband, Jimmy, hung back at a respectful distance, waving at me. He too had long grey hair, a beard and moustache so overgrown I couldn't tell if he smiled.

The worst was over. The moment I describe every time someone finds out I've met my birth mother. "What was it like the first time you saw one another?" they inevitably ask. And I tell them. Sort of.

Pat gripped her door handle as Jimmy drove to the Motel 76 along the Interstate, where we waited out the darkness to drive into the mountains at first light.

I don't tell anyone how it all became pretty normal after that. We got ice from the ice dispenser and Dr. Pepper from the vending machine.

Jimmy propped himself up against the pillows and flicked through television channels until he found a football game. Lee jumped up beside him.

Pat and I peeked out at one another from beneath our turtle shells, still waiting for the right moment. We sipped Dr. Pepper while sitting on top of the blankets of the other bed. I pretended I liked football. When the lights went out and Jimmy began to snore, I stared up at the ceiling. Pat kept shifting on her side of the bed; she was awake too. I was more nervous than I'd been on any first date. Much more.

"You know," Pat whispered, "I've thought about you every day for twenty-three years." She turned towards me. "Every single day."

I turned towards her too. And we stayed like that, silent, waiting for our eyes to adjust to the darkness. Waiting to see a familiar face.

"It's in your blood," she whispered. "Don't let anyone tell you otherwise."

"What's in my blood?"

"The gypsy spirit. I can see it in your eyes."

"I have the same eyes as you." And I did. It was eerie to be staring into my own face. Eerie yet comforting at the same time.

"I'll tell you everything soon," she promised. "I'll tell you where you're from."

ENTERING THE CAVERN

OUR FOUR-PERSON CREW – Rob, Dale, Michel and I – entered the emerald twilight. The heady scent of conifers filled the air. Here, in the shelter of the trees, the rain stopped pouring, the wind stopped howling. Occasional droplets fell from strands of moss and plonked on the forest floor. The trees were so tall, we could barely perceive the lashing of their crowns in the wind. Early morning light flickered like votive candles through the canopy of yellow cedar, western hemlock and Douglas fir. We had come here, to the wilderness of northern Vancouver Island in February of 1996, to pan for gold, but instead we'd been offered a job searching for caves.

Rob, our boss, unfurled a topographical map. We planned our route. He pulled out his plot cord and positioned us a hundred metres apart in a search line. We were armed with compasses, whistles, and waterproof notebooks. Michel kissed my cheek, and walked to his position. In four hours, we'd meet for lunch. He gracefully scissor-jumped a rotting log. He turned and looked at me one last time, as he did each time we parted, and waved.

Trees as wide as two people spread-eagled hid us from each other's view. My compass had been wonky lately, so I was positioned inside, rather than on an outer edge, in case I got lost. Getting lost was easy to do. Thousands of years of design were at work here to attain such a seamless uniformity. Colour palettes blended together subtly. Great swaths of earth-toned mosses draped across the bones of the forest.

I should have felt nervous in a forest that few but the original Indigenous inhabitants had explored. But I didn't. As instinctively as the salmon returned every year to spawn, I'd been migrating from foreign travels and Montréal to the bush of British Columbia every spring for five years, since the twentieth birthday I'd spent in a tree planting camp north of Prince George. I felt more at home here than anywhere else.

It was comforting to know, however, that every fifteen minutes, the furthest left in line would call "Cuckoo!" Each of us, in turn, would call back. This foolproof system, we'd convinced ourselves, ensured that we walked at the same speed and wouldn't surprise any bears. Bears didn't like surprises.

Our whistles were reserved for a higher purpose – three short blows would herald the discovery of what we'd all been praying for: a cave system deserving conservation. Such a discovery would ensure that this stand of old growth wouldn't become what we'd driven through for two hours to arrive here: a clear-cut.

"Cuckoo!" Rob called. We responded and began to walk.

I was looking for cave clues: sinkholes, springs, dry valleys, rock bridges. Mainly, I was listening for the sound of running water, for subterranean flow – major sunken watercourses that flowed underground connecting cave systems. I squeezed between walls of grooved bark. I climbed hillocks and crossed streams. I recorded anything of promise. Rob was convinced we were going to hit it big today. We'd been searching for days and had yet to blow the whistle that would announce a find.

We'd called three sets of cuckoos, but I hadn't recorded anything about caves. Fiddleheads were ready for picking. Thickets of waxy salal leaves promised good berries. I felt distracted. I kept thinking of Michel's face as he'd waved to me. I'd wanted to call out to him, to lie down together on a spongy bed of moss and forget about the world encroaching upon us from beyond the forest line. Our contract here would end next week, and our future remained uncertain.

I was descending a slight slope. A clearing as wide as a two-way bike path ribboned down into a valley – an elk highway, something I'd heard of, but never seen. I noted bear scat. A cluster of primrose. I checked my compass. I followed the path for a few degrees. I felt as though I was walking in the ancient Babylon of forests. Antiquity curled from the boughs in wisps of mist.

It had been a while since I'd heard the crew. "Cuckoo!" I called. Silence. I called again. I moved a few steps south, a few north. The needle on my compass remained still. I did as I'd been trained and found a comfortable spot, sat down, and waited.

But something was watching me. I gripped my whistle, frightened until I recalled that bears could smell fear. I tried to calm down, and breathed deeply. I closed my eyes and inhaled a silence rarer in today's world than any cave system.

This morning at breakfast Dale had said, "It ain't sane to live anywhere you can't piss off the front porch." With a jolt, I realized that he was right.

Michel wanted to return to Montréal, the true love of his life. It wasn't only my compass that was in need of calibration; I needed to take a new inner bearing to discover my own set of coordinates. I'd followed Michel through every possible angle of three hundred and sixty degrees since we'd first met. It was time to stop. I was more frightened of losing myself in his city than in this wilderness.

I heard a faint call coming from the east. Soon my crew appeared. Michel told me I looked scared. And I was. I had to make a choice. "You're in a valley," Rob said, "We couldn't hear you." He looked towards the valley floor and decided to change route. We positioned ourselves closer together this time. I tried to snatch glimpses of Michel in the gaps between trees, but could only hear his presence: the crack of branches, his silly variations of "Cuckoo!" Usually, these made me laugh. Usually, I tried to be just as funny. Now, my call was just loud enough for the sound to carry and echo back, hollow-sounding. I walked quickly. I saw a patch of horsetail. A moss-lined spring.

After about an hour, I heard it – the muffled sound of rushing water. I felt the vibration underfoot, and followed the sound of the invisible river. I climbed a rock face covered in hanging ferns and lichens, and found it on the other side – a limestone archway as wide as a truck. I stood there, looking into the darkness for a few moments, before I blew the whistle.

2546 WEST THIRD

THIRTY-THREE YEARS OLD. Single. Childless. In the past five years I'd slept with a tango teacher, carpenter, guitarist, elementary school teacher, forestry student, architect, cook, urban planner, radio announcer, Trinity College scholar. I'd been employed as a gardener, hotel receptionist, maid, waitress, pottery teacher, cook, piano teacher, busboy, olive picker, hostel manager. I'd called my father from payphones in Kingston, Heraklion, Lisbon. "I'm stuck," I'd said each time.

2546 West Third was the house with a headless black plastic mannequin on the porch. It was a bedsit; nine tenants shared three bathrooms and no one vacuumed the tatty carpet leading up the creaky stairs to my room in the southwest corner. We all had our own kitchenettes, formerly the closets of the family that had lived in this beachside Vancouver neighbourhood in the early 1900s.

The walls were thin. The pipes old. The whole place stunk of cat urine and damp plaster. I burned a lot of Nag Champa. But the rent was cheap and the lease was month-to-month, and it was close to the university. A year ago I'd decided it was finally time to go to university.

I'd been getting tired. Tired of the kinds of jobs that made my back ache. And I'd been feeling embarrassed every time someone asked me what I did and I answered: I'm a waitress. A maid. A gardener. A dishwasher. It was becoming as difficult as the "Where are you from?" question. Passports made it sound so simple. Angela from Canada. Angela from Oshawa. Angela conceived in an olive grove in Italy.

Or so I liked to imagine. Pat never actually told me where I'd been conceived during the hours we spent sitting at her kitchen table while she smoked unfiltered Camels and drank coffee.

"Your father convinced me to meet him in London and travel throughout Europe in a VW van with two farmers from Saskatchewan," she said. "It was like the *Odyssey*."

"Why?"

"We were so broke. We ended up stuck on the island of Sardinia, camped in a swamp with the oxen. We walked the entire length of the island, stealing oranges from people's trees for food." She took a long drag of her cigarette. "Your father's a writer too, you know. Or he was going to write, something to do with rabbits, a social commentary of sorts."

"I'm not a writer."

"Not yet," she said. "Have you ever been to Guatemala?"

"Yes."

"Thought so. Can you still rent a hammock in Tikal?"

"Yes."

Turned out we've been to most of the same places, at nearly the same age.

"And I bet you've been up north in B.C., to the Queen Charlotte Islands."

"No, I haven't." But Michel had been. Planting. Two of our friends had named their daughter Tlell after a place on the archipelago they'd fallen in love with.

"You'll go there someday."

"I really want to go to India," I said.

Pat sipped her black coffee. "That's not a place for the faint of heart."

The last time I saw Pat, she'd driven from her parents' house in Ottawa to where I'd been living with Michel in Montréal. She'd never liked him, even after he'd ridden his mountain bike from Nelson, B.C. to her home in Arizona to beg my forgiveness after his affair with a tree planting cook. Once Pat sent me a letter containing two words: Leave him.

But how could I? I defended his behaviour: He'd grown up with a schizophrenic mother who had been admitted so often to the psychiatric hospital his family had lost count. *"Viens ici, mon ange. Bénis-moi. Protèges-moi,"* she'd say when we'd visit. I'd look toward Michel. He'd nod. I'd touch her. She'd seize my hand and squeeze. "Promise you love me, angel. Promise."

"I promise," I'd say, but she wouldn't let go. She'd pull me so close I could smell her fishy breath, see her skin – so sallow and pocked, such oversized pores. One of her eyes wandered, always looking sideways, towards the maple trees outside the window.

I thought of his mother in the kitchen of the three-bedroom apartment where his six-person family had grown up close to a highway overpass in Montréal, its curtains stained yellow from cigarette smoke. She had just knit me a pair of mittens – thumbs misshapen, cuffs already beginning to unravel. She'd been taking her medication. Her stomach was bloated, her hair falling out. But she could talk. She told me a story of a village outside Trois-Rivières: a house with nine children, a widowed mother who goes to the priest and asks for help, a priest who replies, "Send me your eldest daughter and we'll see what we can do." Her hand shook in mine.

I loved Michel. Simply and completely. I could no more imagine living without him than without my right arm.

Besides, he had always come through – once all was said and done. He was a master of the grand gesture. He'd flown across continents to ask me back after he'd called it quits. He'd woven me willow baskets in the shape of a cornucopia. He'd written "I love you" a thousand times in microscopic script on a piece of bristol board.

Now Pat stood at the door of our apartment on rue de Bordeaux – coincidentally, a block away from where my biological grandparents had lived for fifteen years when they first got married. "I'll probably never be able to do this again," she said as she gave me an envelope filled with ten crisp hundred-dollar bills. "Leave him."

THE PHONE CALL

THE PHONE ON MY BEDSIDE table rang. Isabelle told me Michel's father was dead. At first I thought she said his father was in love. My French was already getting rusty. *Amour. Mort.* Not much of a difference really. "Just thought you'd want to know," she said.

Isabelle and I were still friends even though Michel and I had split in 1998. I looked at the rowan tree outside, the bright orange of its berries. "Would you mind giving me his new phone number?" I asked. She hesitated. Funny how she had become the guardian of his privacy. An old high school friend he saw once or twice a year now, on St-Jean-Baptiste Day or at a thirtieth birthday party. I'd been Michel's girlfriend for nearly seven years. I'd hitched with him from the border of the Yukon to the border of Mexico, cycled from Arizona's White Mountains to the golden gates of San Francisco, cycled from Nelson, B.C. to El Paso, Texas. We'd driven across Canada twice. Planted trees for six seasons. Together we'd panned for gold, searched for caves, picked salal leaves, picked raspberries, taught English, volunteered at soup kitchens, worked as camp counsellors and telemarketers.

"Careful of that gang," my father had warned when he'd realized things with Michel were serious. It was the time of the Referendum when the Québécois were asked to decide whether or not to separate from the rest of Canada. "They're probably a bunch of separatists." And they were. They hung blue and white flags emblazoned with *fleurs-de-lys* from the balconies of their third-floor apartments in the Plateau. They wore T-shirts that said "*Oui!*" and drank beers with apocalyptic names like *La Fin du Monde* and *Maudite*.

They rolled enormous cone-shaped spliffs filled with dope and tobacco – *un bat* – and sat on splintery hardwood floors, playing songs of revolution on the guitar. Their favourites were by a singer named Shawn Phillips, a Texan. They knew all his lyrics by heart and could even sing with the same southern twang. It didn't matter whether or not they understood the words; they understood the sound of passion.

I didn't tell them my parents were part of the "No!" crowd. My mother wanted to ride the "Unity Bus" to Place du Canada and chant, "My

Canada Includes Quebec!"

The separatists accepted me. Kissed me on both cheeks. Fed me *tourtière* and *tarte au sucre*. Offered me homemade cherry brandy and porto flips, their grandmothers' recipes from France. They accepted me because I was Michel's girlfriend, because I made a half-assed effort to speak French, because I was of Irish ethnicity.

"It's in your blood to hate the English too," they'd say, passing me *un bat.*

"But most of the English in Canada aren't even English," I'd say, passing *le bat* to someone else, too nervous to take a drag. "Maybe they speak English but their ancestors could be from Poland, Italy. They don't have a drop of English blood in them."

Michel would coo, "*Mon beau petit chou.*" My beautiful little cabbage. Then he'd squeeze my thigh, the rest of the gang too stoned to understand my muddled French. But Isabelle would nod intently, acting as though I were completely bilingual. Iza and I became fast friends.

I held the receiver to my ear. Iza was still silent. We usually tried to avoid the topic of Michel in the interest of preserving our friendship. "Did he tell you not to give me his number?" I snapped. "His father just died, Iza."

Iza sighed. Even her sigh sounded French. Sexy. She was one of those French women who managed to look fabulously stylish even at minus twenty, whose nose never seemed to go red. She shimmered like a string of Christmas lights against a monochrome sky while I plodded along in sensible boots, wool, and Gore-Tex, blending in with every drab cloud.

Maybe she was sleeping with Michel now. Why not? Maybe she'd had a secret crush on him since the high school years, the guy with electric blue eyes and thick mane of curly black hair who was always forgetting something – a pen, his textbook. Tapping her on the shoulder. Sprawling his lanky legs in the aisle.

I could hear Iza take a pull of a joint. She exhaled. "Don't tell him I gave it to you."

I looked at the number on the piece of paper. I held it to my chest. Don't think about it too much. Just call, it's no big deal. If you make it a big deal, it'll be a big deal. Just call. But it was getting late. There was a time difference. And it was Saturday night. Did I want him thinking I was home alone on a Saturday night? I put the paper beneath my pillow and went to bed.

~

THAT WAS THE YEAR MY FATHER began to lose his memory. Sometimes he'd ask, "Where's Michel?" I said I didn't know. But I knew everything. He had a website. He lived just blocks away from our old place in the Plateau-Mont-Royal. He had a pottery studio and gave lessons. The past threw espresso cups and *bols à café* on YouTube. I could look at Michel's hands, those same hands. I thought his short hair suited him.

More than half a decade had passed since I'd first left Montréal. But I never really left Michel.

By the time he'd arrived home (after a night spent who knows where) on the morning I drove away from rue de Bordeaux, the car had already been packed. Two cats. A pair of cork boots. Half a dozen *huipiles* – hand woven Mayan blouses. It was difficult to choose what to keep from nearly seven years of a life together.

The day before, Michel had kicked in the door on his way out. *"Merde!"* His eyes had darkened. "I wish I could hit you. I just want to hit you right now."

By this point, it had been three summer months since he'd told me he wanted to try a different flavour of ice cream: "I've loved vanilla for many years, but now I want to try strawberry, maybe chocolate."

I'd told him to get out. But he wouldn't leave. He'd come and he'd go. And I'd let him. One day I was the love of his life, the next I was the bane of his existence. He wasn't the only one who was confused. I was good at living in denial. I'd read somewhere that adopted children had major issues with rejection, but hadn't yet understood I was classic case-study material.

"Don't leave!" Michel had yelled from the fire escape when he finally realized what was going on. "Don't leave!" I heard his voice echo as I drove down the back alley, rolling up the window, heading west. I drove fast, not caring about things like speeding tickets or accidents.

After weeks of desperate phone calls at my parents' house in Oshawa, I returned to find Michel waiting for me at Iza's place. He took my hand in his, brought me to his new apartment where we made love on our old futon as though nothing had happened. I had a few days of bliss before I found the love letters from Ingrid. Then I knew I had to leave the country to leave him. But even then I called him from every location in Europe, where I survived by working on farms, waitressing, cleaning hostels – living in a thatch cottage on Inis Mór, a monastery in Rome, an olive grove in Crete, a sheep farm in Pays Basque. And I'd returned to Montréal – to visit Iza, I'd tell myself – again and again.

When I shared these tales, friends and family no longer felt sorry for me. Maybe I'd slept on people's couches one too many times, or stared listlessly at one too many plates of food. Instead of viewing my behaviour as tribute to a man who'd loved me so fully I couldn't live without him, my friends had viewed it as evidence of Michel's controlling and manipulative nature. They perceived me as a hapless victim, systematically destroyed, transformed from a fun-loving, mentally well-adjusted young woman to a cynical, irresponsible basket case.

"You used to be so intelligent," my father had said when Michel and I had still been together and Dad had realized that being in love, becoming a transient, and boycotting higher education weren't just phases. "You were an honours student. Do you know Mr. Beharel, your old English teacher, still asks about you: 'What's that Angela Long doing these days? I always thought she had such potential.'"

~

I DIALED THE NUMBER. *"Allo, vous-êtes bien chez Michel."* I hung up. Dialed again. I closed my eyes, letting his voice sting like salt water in a wound. *"Vous-êtes bien –"* How good it felt to hear his voice. I dialed again.

"Allo? Allo?" I held the receiver tight to my ear. "Angie, is that you?" How good it felt to hear him say my name. "What do you want, Angie?" Why was he so angry with me? His father had just died. I just wanted to express my condolences. "Stop calling me. I know it's you. How many times have you called? Twenty? What's wrong with you?"

I hung up. I looked down at the phone like it was a live creature. I couldn't do this anymore. I had to stop.

GET UP AND SPIN

"THE EARTH HURTLES THROUGH SPACE at a speed of 108,000 kilometres per hour," Ben Pfeiffer said. I stopped chewing my muffin. Ben, a faerie-like woman from the south of France, continued, "Imagine the Sun the size of a Cadillac and the Earth the size of a grape."

After class I wandered around for the rest of the day in a daze, the spell of the universe cast upon me. I felt very small. I wondered if "Exploring the Universe" had been a wise choice as the final course of my Fine Arts degree. Was ignorance really bliss? How comforting it would have felt to believe the earth was flat and stationary, celestial bodies spinning placidly about the stars – deities, sailing across the heavens in barques, their predictable motions determining our fate. But the cornflower-blue summer sky was really just a random scattering of gas molecules; the dusky-rose sunset nothing but the result of an "earth spin." I was living on a glorified rock, hurtling through a void, yet acted like this was all normal. And I wasn't alone.

More than seven billion earthlings walked around, so self-assured and complacent. Did they know over fifty thousand asteroids bumped around in the Kuiper Belt just itching for their chance to break free of their orbit and scream towards Earth? Chunks of rock and metal could do serious damage while travelling at millions of kilometres an hour. According to Ben, NASA tracked ninety percent of what they referred to as Near Earth Objects with radii larger than one kilometre, but didn't bother with the rest, like the one with a radius slightly less than one kilometre that had wiped out 250,000 square kilometres of the Siberian taiga in 1908. Ben said, "We'd have a three-second warning if one were to hit."

How could I think about such things, then iron a black work shirt, tie on an apron, and ask, "Would you like anything to drink to start?" It was difficult to look a customer in the eye when I'd learned that Joni Mitchell was right – they were made of stardust, every one of their atoms built in the core of a star. As I uncorked their bottle of wine and looked towards False Creek at the full moon rising – that was actually the position of the moon's orbit in relation to the earth's rotation – it was difficult not to mention that Pink Floyd was wrong. There was no dark side of the

31

moon. The moon rotated synchronously, always showing the same side to the Earth. The moon was only dark when other entities cast shadows upon it. Often, I wanted to tell them, I felt the same way when I arrived at work, filled with the light of the universe only to be told that my shirt was too wrinkly and table five needed water. Shadow meant -233 degrees Celsius, bright meant +123 Celsius. The universe, I wanted to tell them, unlike their banal conversation, was a place of extremes. But customers didn't want to hear this. They wanted their Gorgonzola Bruschetta.

I understood now why I had troubles keeping up with things. Why when my section filled all at once and every customer glared at me as though they'd just crossed the Sahara by foot rather than ridden the elevator of their million-dollar condo, I wanted to push the pause button. Though gravity tethered us, surely we must have sensed things were moving far too fast. I knew now why when I drank too much, or fell too much in love, I got the spins: my senses gave in, my atoms joined their stardust friends in a cosmic whirling dervish. I tried to let go, but I couldn't. I just wanted it to stop. I wished I'd said no to that last double vodka and cranberry, that I could find a nice, quiet man who just wanted to stay home and do crosswords. I wished I could stand fixed on an immovable axis, like the wind-up ballerina with powder blue tutu stuck to the top of the jewellery box I'd had as a child. Or, at the very least, I wished I could control the turning of that golden crank.

For years, I'd dabbled in yoga, essential oils, and herbal teas, hoping to tether myself to a solid core, to escape the spin. Now I feared it was all a farce – there was no such thing as solidity. Tectonic plates were shifting, lava was rising. The Earth was as young and unruly as a wild colt. Everything was bucking, whinnying, writhing, expanding, contracting, bubbling, cooling, rippling, crashing. Nothing on this planet was solid or fixed; if it were, we'd be dead.

So there was nothing to do but spin. Nothing to do but run from the kitchen to table eight to the bar to table twelve to the patio to the hostess stand to the dishwasher, and smile like a maniac. There was nothing to do but relinquish control to the mysterious forces of the universe, to throw up my hands and laugh at that shiny-faced man at table thirteen who was angry because there were no more soup toasts, or the heavily made-up woman at table nine who had been waiting five minutes for her double-skim latté light on the foam with one shake of cinnamon. I wanted to tell her five minutes didn't even register on a geological time scale where human beings had existed for thirty-five minutes, that we'd waited more than a million years to see the light of Vega scintillate in the summer sky.

I wanted to tell them all that Alan Cromer thinks "science is a new factor in human existence that goes against the grain of our egocentric mind." It was useless to care about soup toasts or coffee when you truly accepted that we, along with the Earth, weren't the centre of the universe, an idea the Catholic Church had also struggled with from 1616 to 1992, when they'd finally crossed Galileo off their list of heretical bad boys. It was challenging to remain egocentric while living on a planet three hundred times smaller than Jupiter, a trillion times smaller than the estimated size of the universe.

I'd begun to wonder if my salvation depended upon embracing my ignorance rather than searching for a solid core of self. Maybe ignorance was my only shot at bliss. According to Ben, even the NASA gang would tell you that most of what we thought we knew was based on conjecture, theories with histories of changing radically from one decade to the next. One tiny discovery could transform our knowledge – or confirm our ignorance – overnight. Any good astronomer knew this, utilizing the realm of the unknown as the blasting pad to explore the unimaginable.

Perhaps the universe was just not as predictable as me. It was an extreme place. Take me to Venus where a day was longer than a year, to Jupiter where the Great Red Spot had stormed for hundreds of years, to Saturn where the wind blew at eighteen hundred kilometres an hour, to Uranus where summer lasted forty-two years. Take me to Pluto where the sun looked the size of a pinhead. Take me to any place that challenged what I once knew, where I could be surprised into transformation. Where I could begin to believe anything was possible.

For how else was a girl to survive the stingy customers of the world – whose idea of a tip was to round their bill of $28.77 to $30.00 – if she didn't believe anything was possible? To believe this in an extreme sense, in an extremity akin to faith? What else did astronomy do but encourage such a faith? It was here I could learn to navigate the unknown, to believe it possible that the woman at table twenty with a fleck of parsley on her front tooth could see through my swirling masses of atoms and realize I too was human and not a robot trained to fetch her a teaspoon that wasn't water stained. It was possible she'd look me in the eye and see that I too was fragile and vulnerable, subject to the whims of an unpredictable universe. I too got parsley stuck between my teeth and could turn into a bitch at the slightest turn of Earth's axis.

It was possible we'd look together towards Cypress Mountain and the black sky would fill with light. We'd watch as the greed, poverty, injustice, and suffering of planet Earth whizzed by at 108,000 kilometres per hour and disappeared back into the void from whence it came. Everyone would put down their forks, get up, and spin. Finally, I would untie my apron and feel immense again: as big as a Cadillac, as powerful as the hydrogen bomb of the Sun whose atoms I shared. I would feel immense because it wouldn't matter anymore that we lived on something the size of a grape, for we were much bigger, more fantastical, than we were capable of imagining.

part two

THE TRAVEL AGENT

I COULDN'T STAY IN DELHI another moment. I couldn't even stay in this country.

"Why change your money to Nepalese rupees?" the travel agent asked.

"Because I'm going to Nepal," I answered.

"Nepal is a bad country. Very dangerous."

"I want to see Everest." Actually, I'd heard Nepal was a gentler place than India, a better place to ease into Asia.

"Oh, but you can see much better than Everest in India. Our Himalayas are Number One. We will take care of everything, Madame. Now I will take you to a secret place to cash your travellers cheques."

Usually I didn't agree to such ventures, but I was simply too hot to argue. After three days of unimaginable heat, my brain was addled. The heat penetrated skin and simmered blood. Cold shower water rolled down my calves as warm as pee. Nothing I wore was light enough or absorbent enough. No fan whirled quickly enough. The fire inside could not be doused and I wandered the city like someone in need of rescue. I must have looked as desperate as I felt.

The travel agent led me through the streets of Paharganj to his friend's shop where travellers cheques were cashed quickly without commission. "They're American dollars, right?" he asked.

I rummaged around in my money belt, feeling flummoxed, even my brain sweating.

"*Shanti, shanti,*" the travel agent said. Peace, peace. "What are you so afraid of?"

I was afraid to disappear down one of those garbage-strewn alleys into a dank cinder-block building and be sold as a white sex slave. I was afraid of being kidnapped by insurgents. I was afraid of getting robbed, raped, of amoebic dysentery.

"Everyone is always staring at me," I said.

"Maybe they think you're beautiful. Or maybe they wonder why you look so afraid. Relax."

I tried my best to heed his advice and release the stomach muscles where my money belt lay plastered by sweat. I tried to look people in the eye. Some of them smiled.

When I'd awoken that morning to the sounds of stray dogs yelping in pain and rage, I'd known my friends and family had been right. "India? Are you crazy?" they'd asked when I told them of my travel plans.

I'd felt invincible the night I'd arrived home from work at two o'clock in the morning, fired up my laptop, and punched the numbers of my Visa card into the British Airways website, declining cancellation insurance. After four years of sitting in university classrooms beneath fluorescent lighting and waitressing in nearly every spare moment, it had been time to go. The hum of my hard drive had said it was now or never. Now, when I was quickly approaching forty and my feet ached from a Friday night of serving wild Pacific salmon on a bed of fiddleheads paired with Okanagan chardonnay. Now, when the sight of anyone drinking five-dollar-take-out lattés, walking designer dogs, and talking on cell phones filled me with loathing. I'd known I was in danger of becoming bitter and cynical. I needed to have faith in something and god wasn't an option.

A euphoric feeling had buoyed me as I began the procedure of closing down my tidy little life: a call to my landlord, a chat with my boss, an email to my parents.

But as my departure date drew nearer my enthusiasm had waned. A taxi driver originally from Mumbai had warned me to wear a false wedding ring and carry bear mace. When I went to the travel health clinic to enquire about vaccinations, the doctor said, "India, hmm? Alone?" He'd looked me up and down. "Which part?"

"Everywhere," I'd answered, a little proudly, scanning the map on the wall from north to south.

The doctor handed me a sheaf of pamphlets: malaria, Japanese encephalitis, typhoid, hepatitis. "Take a look at these and decide how you want to protect yourself."

I read of spastic paralysis, delirium, orthostatic hypotension, and seizures until I was terrified to go. Especially alone. But there was no one to join me. All possible candidates were married with children, expecting more children, in debt, tied to a job, getting laser treatment on their eyes, or simply not interested in the discomforts of travel. But it had been too late to change my plans. I was going to India even if it killed me.

"*Chai!*" the travel agent yelled out into the bustling alleys of Paharganj, and minutes later a little boy returned balancing a tray laden with slender glasses.

"Kashmir will be cool this time of year," the travel agent promised as I handed over a pile of freshly exchanged Indian rupees for a one-way Deccan Air flight and week-long stay on his family's houseboat – a deal my guidebook warned would be a scam of the highest order. I didn't care. This man could have promised me anything so long as I didn't have to clip on my backpack and face the steamy chaos of over twenty million people and thirty thousand wandering cows.

He'd thrown in a complimentary lunch, rickshaw tour, and a place to spend the night. "My sister and her family are visiting from Australia and I know they'd love to meet you. I'll call them right now."

The travel agent must have smelled a sucker. He must have known it had taken me more than twenty-four hours after my arrival at Indira Gandhi International Airport to leave my hotel room. I'd lain on the bed in the middle of the room, overhead fan on high, scarcely able to bear the weight of the sheet. I'd lain there listening to the call to prayer, to Hindi dance music, to praying and chanting, to the breeze blowing through a thicket of trees. I'd smelled the wood-smoke from the Tibetan refugee camp, the stench of sewage wafting across the Yamuna River.

I'd ordered room service – Tibetan *momos*, Chinese stir fry, continental breakfast – the Wongdhen House insignia on everything from the teacups to the fuchsia napkins. I'd wondered if I could stay in this room until my return flight next April. I liked Wongdhen House, its dilapidated elegance. I liked the white marble floors, carved wooden doors, the windows with intricate bars and screens.

But the time had come to either leave the room or catch the next flight home. I remembered the words of my tree planting foreman so many years ago: "Go big or go home!"

"First time in India?" the only other lone traveller sitting in the Wongdhen House restaurant asked.

Was it so obvious? "Yes," I said, wondering which would be safer – the porridge or the banana pancakes.

"This is my tenth visit to Mother India," the traveller said. "Don't worry, she grows on you."

I took a bite of a banana pancake, hoping the oil of oregano I'd taken as parasite protection would save me from its uncooked centre. "The Metro isn't far from here. Brand spanking new. Great way to get into town." He explained how to get to the subway. I secretly hoped he'd offer to go with me. I looked around the crowded dining room at the other tourists sitting in groups of two or three, laughing over cups of honey-lemon-ginger tea, reading the pages of their guidebooks with relish.

But after three days of subways, autorickshaws, Ambassador cabs, and cycle- rickshaws, Mother India still hadn't grown on me. I'd never been anywhere dirtier, noisier, more chaotic. There were no lines on the road. "We talk with our horns!" an autorickshaw driver bragged. I'd never seen such poverty: women begging with what looked like dead babies in their arms, whole families living in tarp shacks on traffic islands, children, maybe three years old, rummaging through piles of garbage and excrement for plastic bottles to salvage. Everywhere I looked lay the potential for heartbreak. So I stopped looking. I kept my head down.

It was like I'd flown to the end of the world; this was what would become of us when all the systems we held dear came toppling down. I'd stood in the centre of a roundabout, stranded until it was clear to cross. I'd watched the chaos swirl around and around, somehow none of it colliding with a sacred cow. I'd waited for it all to explode or implode or even just stop for a moment and take a breath. But it hadn't. "A functioning anarchy," was how a friend with a penchant for politics had described it with admiration.

The travel agent called out into the alley again, and this time another young boy appeared with a stack of round stainless steel containers. "Lunch time," the travel agent said. He must have noted the surprise on my face. "Anything you want in India, any time, it's yours. Like magic."

"If you have money," I said.

"Well, that is never a worry for you westerners."

I felt like telling him I was not one of those westerners. Money was always a worry. I remembered standing in line at a natural foods store in Vancouver just last year, with just enough to buy an onion and a head of garlic. I'd watched the woman in front of me with envy as she unloaded a cart filled with organic foodstuffs: yellow-fleshed mini watermelons, discs of soft unripened cheese decorated with pressed flowers. I'd slept for a month on a camping mattress on my apartment's splintery hardwood floor until I graduated to a futon mattress on the floor, imagining my neighbours in their multi-million dollar renos sleeping on 500-thread-count Egyptian cotton sheets. But when I looked around me here, I knew the travel agent was right. Just the fact I had a passport and could afford a flight ticket was enough to place me in the category of extreme privilege.

We ate *dal* and *chapatis* and the questions began: "Where are you from?" "Are you married?" "Do you have children?" "Do you have brothers? Why did they leave you alone?"

After lunch, the rickshaw tour, and the bonus cappuccino at a swank café (where mating couples meet in secret, the travel agent joked), I prepared to meet my doom at his apartment.

But his sister was there, waiting with her husband and three children and a feast they'd prepared in my honour. We sat on cushions. We ate curries laced with plump raisins and cashews. We drank apricot juice and Kashmiri *chai*. Soon the sun set red and fiery in the polluted skies of Delhi. Soon we moved the cushions and rolled out the mattresses. We slept side by side. We farted and snored and dreamed together until it was time to wake up and send me off to the airport.

At four in the morning, the city was already awake. Cows wandered from one garbage heap to another, rickshaw-*wallahs* lit incense for their dashboard gods. I was already sweating. The travel agent flagged down an Ambassador cab and paid my fare. I realized I still didn't know his name.

"You have Delhi family now," he said and gave me his business card. "Any problem, anywhere in India, you call."

THE WOODCARVER

THE WOMEN CAME EVERY MORNING, perched on the prows of wooden boats with colourful scarves tied around their heads. They dipped long oars into the lake and glided towards the marsh. I opened the shutters of my room and watched them disappear into the reeds, calling to one another like songbirds. They collected lotus leaves to feed the cows, to keep the milk sweet. I heard the slap of giant leaves on water as they shook mud from the roots.

The sun breached the mountains. Javed would be here soon with my breakfast and I still wasn't dressed. I was the only guest staying on The Mughal-E-Azam Houseboat, the only person who had stayed there in quite some time. Tourism had waned since insurgents kidnapped six western hikers in 1995 and one of them was found beheaded with the words "Al Faran" carved into his chest. But the turmoil in Kashmir had begun long before. India and Pakistan had been fighting for control of Kashmir since 1947. From 1989 to 2004, most of the state was closed to visitors due to violent unrest, and the Canadian government regularly issued an advisory to avoid all travel to the former "tropical Switzerland of Asia" that was plagued by grenade attacks, landmines, and bombings. The Indian government had designated Kashmir, a predominantly Muslim state in a predominantly Hindu nation, a "disturbed area." But the travel agent in Delhi had assured me not to worry.

"Governments like to exaggerate," he'd said. "My brother will meet you at the airport. You'll be perfectly safe."

Javed was the eldest son of the Shalla family, the fourth-generation owners of the Mughal-E-Azam. He'd spent all of his thirty-five years on this lake and had learned to speak several languages fluently during the days when Kashmir was touted as "Paradise on Earth." Those were the days when waterways were the only roadways, and *shakira* floated past gardens filled with musk melon and water chestnuts, carrying mulberries and saffron from the surrounding villages, and a people who had lived this way, nestled in the Vale of Kashmir, for centuries.

"When the British Raj came and saw Kashmir, they wanted it," said Javed. "But it wasn't for sale. They weren't allowed to buy the land."

But they could buy the houseboats. They filled them with crystal

41

chandeliers and sterling silver tea services, then sold them back to the original owners when it was time to leave India. Javed showed me letters from former guests – staff of the British High Commission, poets he told me were famous, Bollywood stars.

"Do you know who this is?" he asked, pointing at a signature. I shook my head, running my finger along the scrawls of name after name.

You wouldn't have known from the condition of the Mughal-E-Azam that tourists were rare. The chandeliers sparkled, the mahogany tabletops gleamed. Every morning Javed delivered my breakfast on a silver tray: a boiled egg, toast, marmalade, a pot of cardamom tea. His mother, whom I'd yet to meet, prepared these in a bungalow on the tiny island to which the boat was moored.

I heard Javed lower the gangplank and slide open the houseboat door, then the clatter of china in the dining room. I would have preferred to eat on the veranda and look at Dal Lake through the ornately carved screens of walnut. But Javed insisted I eat in the dining room, sitting at a table for ten with my feet on the finely woven Kashmiri carpet. He sat in the corner of the room and watched me, ready to attend to my every need. He rarely smiled.

I sat down and took a sip of tea. The slap of lotus leaves on water drifted in through the windows.

"Is it sweet enough?" he asked.

I nodded.

"What are your plans today?"

"I don't know," I answered. Every day for the past week Javed had suggested various tours of local sights: the Mughal gardens, a cable car ride to the peaks of Gulmarg.

I spread marmalade on my toast. Javed watched from his chair. The women glided past the window, boats piled high with leaves.

"Today is the first day of Ramadan," he said.

"Does that mean you're fasting?"

"Of course," he said, and stood to collect my dishes.

Later I sat on the velvet-cushioned bench on the veranda while the sun edged its way around the lake, and I admired the carved wooden screens. Every day I saw something new hidden in their design: the wings of a bird, the petals of a flower. Javed appeared on the gangplank with a silver tray laden with tea and cookies. He sat on the other cushioned bench and stared out at the water.

"Is it sweet enough?" he asked.

I nodded, then opened my book and read, hoping he'd get the hint.

"What are you reading?" he asked.

I held up the book: *The Story of My Experiments with Truth*, by Mahatma Gandhi.

"What's it about?"

"India," I answered. "The independence of India."

He continued to stare out at the water. A kingfisher dove into its calm surface.

"I never learned how to read," he said.

The sun rounded the houseboat, and I shifted to face it head-on as I told Javed what I'd read of Gandhi's early life.

"Do you know who did these carvings?" he asked when I paused. He bent to refill my cup. "I did," he said. "During the war."

"Did you do the ones inside too?"

"All of them," he said. "It was a long war."

I asked to look at the other woodcarvings again, with the artist by my side. We walked through the entire houseboat. The chair legs, the mirror frames, even the carved ceiling panels, were all his handiwork.

"The schools were closed down. There was nothing else to do," he explained. I ran my finger along a tendril of a vine. "I was too young to fight," he said. "And so I carved."

THE CARPET SELLER

THE BUS STARTED ITS ENGINE. A young man wearing the long woolen cape typical of Kashmiris slid into the seat beside me.

"My name is Amir," he said. "A pleasure to meet you." He was delighted we were both headed towards the same final destination, Leh, a two-day journey up the Zojila Pass and through the Indus Valley. There he would join his uncle to close up the family carpet shop for the season.

"Did you know Kashmiris weave the best carpets in the world?" he asked.

I smiled politely, bracing myself for the sales pitch, but Amir just looked out the window.

I watched as the streets of Srinagar were transformed from a warren of fruit stalls and butcher shops into a city under siege: machine gun emplacements, barbed wire, camouflage netting. Indian army commandos fanned out to man the posts.

"What's happening?" I asked.

"Don't worry," Amir said, "they never shoot the tourists."

We waited as last-minute passengers loaded their cargo onto the roof of the bus: large burlap sacks of rice, boxes secured with string, forty-gallon tins of mustard oil. The roof shook with the impact. Amir unfolded the *Srinagar Times*.

"Do you mind if I read?" he asked.

On the front page, I noticed a photo of a burnt-out car surrounded by graceful Arabic script. "What happened?"

He flipped to the next page. "*Shanti, shanti.*"

I shifted on the ripped green vinyl, trying to get comfortable on the converted school bus that would soon transport us along one of the most dangerous roads in the world. Not only did its one-laned, mostly unpaved track snake through the heights of the Himalayas, but it hugged the disputed Pakistani-Indian border, otherwise known as the Line of Control. Shellings and hijackings were regular occurrences. But of course, I'd skipped that part of the *Lonely Planet* and knew none of that at the time.

This was the only available route to Leh – or so I'd been told – and the fabled Himalayan Kingdom of Ladakh, a land of benevolent Buddhists perched on a high-desert plateau ringed by snow-capped peaks. A land, I hoped, of peace and quiet.

"What do you do in your country?" Amir asked.

I hesitated. Just a few weeks ago I was a waitress with a creative writing degree working at a restaurant called Fiddlehead Joe's. "I'm a writer," I answered, to simplify things.

"A journalist?"

"Kind of."

"Dangerous job," he said and returned to the newspaper.

I glanced over to see a photo of a man with a gunny sack over his head tied at the neck with a rope. I started to feel nervous. I scanned the faces of the passengers on the bus to discover I was the only woman. But none of the men seemed to pay me any heed. They were all too busy reading.

The driver started the bus. "Ladakh! Ladakh!" he yelled one last time into clouds of diesel fumes.

It wasn't long before we began to climb the Himalayas at much too sharp an angle. We cut through cliff faces and avalanche zones. We shot down mountain passes, across washouts. There were no guardrails or brake checks or runaway truck lanes. Instead, hand-painted signs decorated rock faces and errant boulders: "If you're married to speed, divorce her"; "After whisky driving risky"; "Keep your nerves on the curves."

We passed road work crews – men mixing tar in cauldrons atop giant smoky fires, women swinging pickaxes, breaking apart boulders with loud clangs. Children carried buckets of rocks on their heads.

"They are from Bihar," Amir told me. "The poorest people of India, but the hardest workers."

At the base of every gorge, remnants of unlucky vehicles glinted in the sunlight. There were times when we teetered on the outermost edge of the road, waiting for military convoys to pass. I watched as rocks fell, gathering speed as they tumbled into oblivion.

We passed through village after village. Checkpoint after checkpoint. I grew accustomed to the soldiers dotting the landscape every few hundred feet. They stood in the middle of alpine meadows, in pastures among the sheep. The Kashmiris went about their business, oblivious, it seemed, to the guns draped so casually across the soldiers' chests.

As the bus limped to the top of a pass, I looked back towards the landscape we'd traversed. There was nothing but wave after wave of mountain peak. I looked ahead to mountains soaring higher than I'd imagined. It was the kind of scene that made me feel like there was nowhere else I'd rather be than right here, right now. On this bus.

Maybe the altitude was making me giddy. Or maybe it was the villages – the half-timbered houses with fretwork eaves, the women wearing headscarves selling bags of apricot kernels and almonds. Maybe it was Amir, the way he bartered on my behalf with the vendors, how he insisted on buying *chai* for me at every rest stop. Maybe it was the way he accompanied me to the checkpoints where soldiers in their India-issue uniforms recorded my passport details inside canvas tents. How he stood there, watching them carefully with a protective look in his eye.

The irony – that after several weeks in India I'd finally begun to relax on one of the most dangerous roads on the planet – didn't escape me. Every bump and jolt of the bus jerked me back to life. And then we stopped.

The other bus passengers didn't seem surprised when, shortly after sunset, the driver turned off the ignition in Kargil and closed his eyes. Amir folded up his paper, and gathered his other belongings.

"What's happening?" I asked.

"We stop here," he said. "It's too dangerous to drive at night."

Where would I go? My *Lonely Planet* guidebook was inside my backpack that was lashed to the roof of the bus. I couldn't see anything around the bus station but cement buildings in various states of construction, and a couple of those banana-yellow phone booths where I'd once managed to call my mother in front of two amused-looking teenage boys.

"Follow me," said Amir. "I know a hotel."

This is what he's been waiting for, I thought. Now whatever he'd been planning since Srinagar would unfold. But what unfolded was a mattress on a metal-framed cot in a female dorm. I was glad the room was lit by dim bare bulbs hanging from the ceiling. I followed the lead of the other women when I used the communal bathroom – taking a deep breath, and rolling up my pant legs.

Amir checked to make sure I was okay.

"Tomorrow morning, 4:30 a.m.," he said. Before India, that had sounded early. But now I knew that by four o'clock in the morning, hundreds of millions of Indians would be starting their days as a matter of course. If you weren't up by that hour, something was wrong with you.

When we reached the top of the final pass the next day, the driver cut the engine. We coasted into the Indus. The sound of an immense landscape swooshed through the windows. We picked up speed, until alpine meadow blurred into high-desert plateau, until nothing behind remained.

We arrived in Leh. Amir shook my hand. I prepared myself for the warnings of my guidebook – friendly companions suddenly recommending tours where a commission awaited them, or demanding a guide fee.

Amir waited by the taxi stand until he found a driver to take me to the Oriental Guest House and paid him in advance. I offered rupees; Amir declined them.

"Thank you for visiting Kashmir," he said. "Will you promise to write about us one day?"

In the bright light of the high desert plateau, I noticed his worn shoes, his duffel bag with torn strap. I watched from the window of the taxi as he walked down a narrow alley, his woolen cape disappearing into the shadows.

THE LONG-TERM GUESTS

AT FIVE O'CLOCK IN THE MORNING, the snow-covered peaks of the Zanskar Range still glowed in the moonlight. Solomon led the way. Carmen and I followed close behind, hesitant to leave Leh's Oriental Guest House in the cold and dark of an October morning. We moved slowly beneath backpacks filled with souvenirs of these lands: antique Tibetan textiles, dried apricots, turquoise pendants.

We descended the hillside. There were no such things as street lights here. Darkness was reserved for creatures with night vision, or flashlights. Mine did little but cast an eerie pool of light on the pot-holed road. Wary of stray dogs, we found rocks to clutch in our right hands, and walked in the middle of the dirt road, knowing full well that neither precaution would save us.

Solomon knew a shortcut to the bus station. It involved walking beyond the touristy part of town where places with names like Hotel Yak Tail, Pumpernickel German Bakery, and Wonderland stood shuttered for the season.

We could have arranged for a taxi, but Solomon frowned upon such frivolities. "A taxi will cost less than a dollar each," Carmen had said. But Solomon prided himself on living like the locals. I suspected, however, the locals knew better than to wander the back alleys of Leh in the middle of the night. Perhaps that's why Solomon seemed unnaturally chipper at this early hour, trying to persuade his two companions what an adventure this was. As I clutched my rock, I couldn't help but notice my heartbeat accelerating. Especially when the light of my flashlight faded, then died. Especially when a pack of stray dogs began to yip and howl.

We kept walking. It was taking longer than we'd planned. None of us voiced our shared fears we'd miss the bus, the bus destined to take us out of the cold mountains and into the hot plains of India. It was the only bus until next week, maybe even next spring, if it snowed again and the pass closed.

To be honest, the thoughts of being stuck in the northernmost tip of India appealed to me. Already I was nostalgic for my room at the Oriental Guest House, with a view of the glaciers and a temple the Dalai

Lama himself had christened *Shanti*. In fact, the guest house would be the perfect place to be stranded. Meals were served twice a day in a sun-drenched garden blooming with cosmos, zinnias, and marigolds. Money never changed hands. Guests ticked off their purchases, honour-system style, on a sheet provided at check-in. The guest house was owned by a family of benevolent Tibetan Buddhists. Wind chimes tinkled in the trees. Grandfather wandered the grounds swinging a prayer wheel.

Roy, from Squamish, B.C., had been there four months and had no plans to leave. He rented a room where a former guest had stayed long enough to finish a mural of the jungles of Maharashtra, covering every bit of wall space. Roy pinned a map of India to the canopy of palm fronds. He studied India every day, marking all places of interest with colourful push pins even though he didn't intend to visit any of them. "Here. There," he chuckled. "What's the difference?"

It had been easy to fall into a rhythm at the Oriental Guest House. Every morning I was awoken by Grandfather saying his prayers. He mounted the stairs to the second floor muttering mantras under his breath, extracting an ancient key from the folds of his robe to open the glass-walled temple across the hall from my room. Every day I became more and more part of the travel stream – a circuitous route revolving around food, transportation, accommodation, banking, hygiene. Where to change money. Where to buy toilet paper. Where to eat *momos*. It was easy to swirl round and round in this eddy. Not many of us could afford such a life of leisure in our own countries. How could any of us think we deserved it? I'd think of all this, and then Grandfather would pass, spinning his prayer wheel.

We walked faster. The yipping of dogs became even more frantic, and closer. We entered a barren field. Unfamiliar constellations stretched overhead. I cursed Solomon under my breath, though I knew how lucky I was to have met him and Carmen. Not many ventured to India's northernmost state in the off-season. This was the season for beach raves in Goa, not trips to the disputed Chinese-Indian border in the Nubra Valley. The chances of a trio of Canadians meeting at the end of a dusty road in Hunder were so miniscule that when it happened we had no choice but to share a jeep back to Leh together.

But I was beginning to think the extraordinary was the ordinary in

India. Even with the whiff of sewage and the sound of scurrying creatures along the edge of the field, I couldn't help but gawk at the stars and the snow-capped peaks glittering in the clarity of Leh's sky. Here, at 13,500 feet above sea level, the air was so thin that the line between this world and the universe beyond had all but disappeared.

I wasn't surprised when we crossed the field and heard the comforting rumble of an idling bus. "We made it!" Solomon cried triumphantly. A *chai* stand emerged from the darkness and Solomon strode up to the counter. "*Chai?*" he asked. Carmen and I looked at the rocks in our hands and laughed.

THE BOY ON THE ROAD

DARKNESS GATHERS BEHIND the belt of the Himalayas. I walk, careful not to step in the ditch filled with fetid water when the autorickshaws pass and we begin to jockey for space on this narrow road. This is India, I think, as a rickshaw swerves around the corner and barrels towards me.

This is India. I squeeze myself alongside the ditch, hoping the driver can see past the tinsel, streamers, and deities decorating his windshield. This is India. I shouldn't be wearing flip-flops. I shouldn't have left my blonde hair hanging past my shoulders. I shouldn't be out this late.

A stray dog snarls. The sky darkens too quickly, blurring the branches of the rhododendron into nothingness. This is India. This is the road women are warned to avoid after sunset. But I haggled too long with the shopkeeper from Kashmir. I drank too many cups of cardamom tea. I clutch the paper bag, think about the moonstone earrings inside.

I see the lights of my hotel twinkling on the hillside. I'm almost there. Almost safe in the town the Dalai Lama and the Tibetan government-in-exile call home. I think about dinner. About a cold Kingfisher at the place with the outdoor terrace. Suddenly, a young boy darts out in front of me and throws something red at my feet. Hot sparks prick my toes. "Boom!" The boy laughs from the other side of the road. He throws another firecracker, then another, and soon I trip into the ditch trying to escape.

This is India. I walk faster, thinking about the contents of my bag instead of the filth on my feet. Lapis lazuli from the mountains of Pakistan. Polished jade.

I remember it's Diwali, the festival of light. The dark sky barely has a moment to relax. Everything is awash in exploding, flickering, blazing light. Doorways open. People dance. They offer exquisite-looking sweets. They smile as though I've travelled twelve thousand kilometres just to meet them here, on this narrow road. In this moment.

This is India. I loosen my grip on the bag, open my hand, and accept a sweet.

THE MONK

THE PARISIANS WERE SMOKING HASH again playing guitar on the terrace. I decided it was a good time to walk to the top of the hill overlooking Dharamsala, where a white temple perched among the pines. I was feeling a bit lost on this subcontinent. Even if I didn't really know why I'd come to this country, I knew it wasn't to eat hummus and pita and get high.

The dog at the hotel followed me as he had for the past few days when I'd walked down the hill to Green Café. Now he led the way up the rocky footpath beside the stream. Many paths converged onto this one, and all manner of characters were said to wander these foothills. There were rumours of bandits, criminals on the run, drug dealers, and misguided American hippies. But I felt safe with the dog at my side. He growled at everyone who crossed our path: a young shepherdess, a Japanese photographer, a lone horse.

The dog stopped to drink from a pool beneath a small waterfall, and I sat on the rocks and watched the butterflies. My companion stopped in mid-gulp, looked up, and unfurled his ears to their mangy tips. Then he trotted off the main path. I followed, mostly because I didn't really have a choice; I'd lost track of all the turns we'd made to get here. The white temple had disappeared. Strings of multi-coloured prayer flags stretched from one pine crown to another.

I soon realized we were following someone. I saw a flash of brick-red robes, a bald head nicked with shaving cuts. A monk. The words of the hotel owner came to mind: "Never trust a monk. Anyone could be hiding beneath those robes."

The path grew steeper, rockier. The monk crossed the stream up ahead, and then looked down towards us. He smiled and turned to shimmy across a shale ridge. The dog followed. I shuffled behind, sending loose rock clattering down the hillside. Finally I stood before an adobe hut, trying to catch my breath. The monk leaned against the doorframe, breathing easily. "*Chai?*" he asked, a smile deepening the lines on his face. He held up a teacup in case I hadn't understood. I smiled and nodded. The dog wagged his tail. The monk pointed to a thin cushion on a stone bench, then stooped through a wooden doorframe carved with symbols.

I sat with the sun on my face and looked out across the foothills. A flock of sheep, shepherded by women in bright saris, zigzagged across the terraced hillside. The monk returned with the *chai*. I took a sip, and he waited for my reaction. "Delicious," I said. From gaps in the wall he retrieved an onion, half a cabbage, a tomato. Then he disappeared inside again.

I drank my *chai*, closed my eyes, and listened to the soft hiss of a gas flame from the hut. When I opened my eyes, the dog had gone. I panicked for a moment, wondering how I'd find my way back. But then I realized it was OK. Suddenly everything was OK. I remembered the words of David while we'd sat in his hut in Guatemala. "Going to India is like taking your head off and putting it back on in the opposite direction," he'd said. "You have to learn how to see again."

Soon a bowl filled with fragrant rice and vegetables arrived. The monk smiled and ducked back into the hut. From the other side of the door, I heard the scrape of spoon against bowl. I ate, too.

THE FIVE-ARMED GODDESS

I DON'T KNOW THE NAMES HERE – the name of the yellow-masked bird, tree with starburst leaves, the leper who begs in front of the fruit stand. I don't know the name of the five-armed goddess dressed in purple velvet and glitter hearts. But I walk uphill to her temple, look into her cracked eye, and ring the copper bell. Sound ripples namelessly along footpaths and foothills, along stitches of page-like flags strung from one nameless branch to another.

THE ORPHAN

I REALIZED I WAS CAGED IN to keep the monkeys out – I saw two of them beyond the steel grid welded to my balcony watching me from the rooftop of the dining hall: a male with a flame-red backside mounting a female. He stopped to examine his penis. She picked lice from his back.

It was disconcerting to be caged in, but I knew there was no other option; monkeys were the rats of India, or so I'd been told. They stole, shamelessly, anything that appealed to their senses – children's ice cream cones, women's rainbow-hued scarves. I'd witnessed one steal a grapefruit right out of the hands of an old lady.

In a town near Dharamsala, I'd been advised by a Spanish woman named Lou to purchase an umbrella – preferably colourful and patterned – to protect myself: "Open it up and 'Poof!' off they go, back to the trees."

But I couldn't find any umbrellas for sale. Supposedly a monsoon inundated this country for at least four months of the year, but I had my doubts. The garden inside the perimeter of the fence consisted of a few dusty rose bushes with a handful of buds that looked as though they'd never bloomed.

I glided my hand along the cage, looking at my palm, the once-smooth skin now crossed-hatched with fine lines. The dryness would take its toll on more than just the roses. I looked at India through the tiny frames of the cage's grid: a side of bus, a flash of wing, a shimmer of water tank.

Suddenly the monkeys began to screech, a high-pitched, frantic screech that sounded nothing like the playful monkey calls of Hollywood films. They swung towards me from the pipes of the water tank to the wires of a power line. The cage shook with the impact of their landing. They bounced across the grid and stopped in front of me, blocking my view of India.

The black pads of their hands gripped the steel, the digits, so like fingers, poking. I touched the locket around my neck that I'd bought from a Tibetan refugee. I caressed the turquoise and red coral, the silver filigree.

"It will protect you, Madame," the Tibetan had promised, "from barrenness and other evils."

Dutifully, I fastened the locket around my neck every morning. It was the closest I'd ever come to having a religion.

The monkeys bared their yellow-stained teeth and shook the cage, screeching. I thought I should try to smile, to show I understood – yes, I was another one of those crazy westerners looking for themselves. But then, halfway through smiling, I remembered what Lou had said about teeth: "Never, under any circumstances," and she'd wagged her umbrella at me, "never show them your teeth. Most importantly, don't smile – they'll think you're provoking them."

Lou was right. The monkeys were outraged. The male with the flame-red backside began to spit at me. Other monkeys began to appear from other rooftops. I touched the locket, as I'd touched it many times since my journey from the Great Himalayas of Leh to the Indo-Gangetic Plains of Haridwar, and felt safe.

Thankfully, the lunch bell rang. I could hear the children gathering to line up and enter the dining hall. I wanted to arrive first to be less conspicuous, even though I knew that was impossible. There were seventy children and me, the lone foreign volunteer, staying at Sri Ram Ashram and Orphanage – school, medical clinic, and "loving home for orphaned and destitute children."

I'd been told it was unfortunate I hadn't arrived a few weeks later when Babaji – monk, master yogi, and founder of Sri Ram – was due to visit, accompanied by his entourage of American followers. Apparently, Babaji preferred to spend India's dry season in Santa Cruz.

"If I were you, Madame," they'd suggested, "I would stay until Babaji returns."

By then I'd heard all about his annual visits – how he gave the children toffees after breakfast and chocolate bars in the late afternoon: "It's like Christmas every day when Babaji is here." I'd heard about the trampoline where he taught the children tricks. How he communicated by white board and black marker and hadn't spoken since 1952. "He blows a whistle if the children are misbehaving."

I'd heard these things with my usual skepticism of all things spiritual. Somewhere at the heart of all these organizations lay a scam, I'd thought.

It was just a matter of time, before their cover was blown.

I hurried away from the balcony, leaving the monkeys to screech at my underthings strung up to dry, and collected my plate and spoon.

In the dining hall I sat cross-legged on the strip of burlap on the girls' side and waited. I examined my stainless steel plate separated into five compartments. Soon it would be filled with rice, *dal*, pickled mango, yogurt – all products of the ashram's sixteen-acre farm.

I polished my spoon with the hem of my *kameez*, a long tunic worn over long trousers called *salwar*. This was the suggested attire here. Preferably white. Upon my arrival, I'd been shown to a large steamer trunk filled with layers of neatly folded *salwar-kameez* and multi-coloured scarves – clothing Babaji's followers had left behind. I'd packed away my khaki trousers and cotton T-shirts, visiting the trunk every morning to choose an outfit.

Today's *salwar-kameez* was lavishly hand-embroidered with flowers and vines. I'd draped a lemon-coloured scarf, a *dupatta*, across my chest to cover my arms just above the elbows and, more importantly, hide my breasts. Even though I was one of those women who'd never really needed a bra, it didn't seem to matter. Breasts had a more symbolic value here than anything else. Any woman who flaunted them (which meant not draping a scarf over them) was asking for trouble.

At the last moment, I slid on a few bangles, and put on some lipstick. Then I caught sight of myself in the mirror and hoped I hadn't overdone it.

The kitchen workers set up for lunch, piling *chapatis* into baskets and stirring fresh curd. A woman in a fuchsia sari splashed with yellow polka dots stopped stirring and looked up. "Oh, that's much better, Madame. Much better. The children will very much like your new look."

The children began to fill the room. Boys first. They sat on their burlap on the other side of the room, facing me, leaning into one another to whisper and giggle.

The girls arrived next, hurrying towards the spot where I sat, vying to be the one who got to sit beside the foreigner and examine, close-up, every detail of my attire, every pore on my face, every move I made.

At first, I'd felt uncomfortable under such scrutiny. But the children examined me with such unadulterated curiosity that I'd grown to enjoy the attention. They touched my hair, held my hand, their eyes never leaving mine, searching through me as I'd been searching through the grid of the cage. And I wondered: What did they see?

Today a thin girl with a slight limp crouched down to sit cross-legged beside me. The others had let her pass, deciding it was her turn. She stared at me. I smiled. The girl caught sight of the locket around my neck. I unclasped it, passing it to her.

"It's okay," I said, watching as the women began to serve the boys. The girl caressed the red coral and turquoise.

"Does it open?" she asked. I nodded. "What's inside? Do the gods live inside?"

I thought for a moment. One of the kitchen helpers arrived with a steaming cauldron.

"Let's open it after lunch and see," I promised as one of my plate's compartments filled with yellow *dal*.

I watched the children scoop perfect portions with cupped palms, pushing the food with a thumb into their mouths, never spilling a single grain of rice. They ate in unison, silently, and with purpose. As I watched, I thought about what the ashram's nurse had told me about the history of some of these children. Who had been beaten and left for dead on a garbage heap in Punjab? Who had arrived with one side of their head flattened? Who had been covered in their own excrement? Who had survived the earthquake buried beneath a pile of dead bodies?

I clasped my spoon and scooped up some *dal*. Only foreigners used utensils here. I'd been advised to keep my spoon in my room. If I lost it, it wouldn't be replaced. But suddenly I wanted to eat with my hands, to feel the rice and *dal* in the cup of my palm. I watched the children's movements.

The girl looked up as I put down my spoon. She smiled. Slowly, she mixed a portion of rice into the *dal*. I followed. Slowly, she cupped her palm. I felt the stickiness of rice, the wetness of *dal*. Together we brought our cupped palms closer to our mouths, grains of rice spilling into my yogurt along the way. The girl smiled as encouragingly as a young mother.

The locket sat between our knees on the burlap. I wished I'd filled it with something, anything – a bead, a pebble. I worried now the girl would be disappointed when she discovered there was nothing inside.

Soon, the compartments on my plate were empty. I picked stray grains of rice off the burlap. I touched the locket.

"May we check now, Madame?" the girl asked. "Please?"

The doors of the dining hall opened. Heat and sunshine streamed in as the children gathered their plates and lined up at the washing stations. I heard the monkeys screeching their way towards the place beside the kitchen where the cooks threw vegetable scraps and fruit peels. As they played tug of war with rubbery *chapatis*, their screeching resembled human laughter even more.

I looked at the girl, suspecting she'd already endured greater disappointments in life than an empty locket. "Go ahead," I said.

Carefully, she opened the clasp and held the locket open by the hinges. "Look, Madame!"

The silver hollows looked dull, unpolished. But a brightness transformed the girl's eyes. It was the look of faith, I thought. She closed the locket and held it out to me.

"Keep it," I said. I knew how easy it would be to find another locket in another town filled with Tibetan refugees.

"Oh, no," the girl said quickly, "you can't give away the gods." She looked at me as though my scarf had just fallen away from my chest. She stood up. "But be careful of those monkeys, Madame. They'll steal it from you the moment they have the chance."

THE SAGE

EVERY DAY, I WALKED FROM Phool Chatti Ashram to the Ganges River for a swim. Along the way, I passed a cave chiselled out of the rock. There was an old man there, a holy man. He was usually crouched low over a fire, snapping twigs. I tried my best not to let him see me looking inside his home. I didn't want to be disrespectful, but I was curious. I'd never seen a holy man's living quarters before. Sometimes, when I thought he was bent low enough, I slowed down to catch a better glimpse of life inside the cave. I saw a battered pot, a wool blanket. I saw an altar at the back: candles burning, pictures of Hindu gods and goddesses. Today the holy man was sitting very still at the mouth of his cave, gazing at the lemon trees. It was difficult not to stare at his long, neatly combed white hair and intense brown eyes.

When I arrived at my swimming spot, I waited behind the rocks until the groups of white-water rafters had bobbed past, then dove straight into water fresh from the Himalayas. The cold was shocking.

At the ashram, they joked I must have had Canadian blood to swim in the Ganges so late in the season. I humoured them, saying I came from a people who ran naked into oceans in subzero temperatures on New Year's Day. To be honest, my blood rebelled against the water temperature. It numbed my every cell.

But the river cured everything, eventually, I'd been told. Rheumatism. Cancer. Snakebites. Broken hearts. Bad karma. For thousands of years people had found their way to its banks and prayed to it, adorned it with flowers, burned their dead beside it, swum in it. Millions and millions of people. I liked to float along in its current, thinking of this. I liked to imagine my body as a sieve and the river straining through me, the rapids crushing any molecules of disease. I liked to imagine my chronically broken heart coming dislodged and floating downstream like a dead branch, my bad karma sinking to the bottom with the silt. Like the silt, every day it seemed to pile higher as I remembered some new misdemeanor: Lies. Jealousy. Unkindness. It was all there. Cringing in the cold water, I thought back on turning thirty, and on my twenties, and all the way back to my teens. I waited for the river to swallow me whole. But it didn't.

After my swim, I walked along the beach and shivered. Sometimes I'd see the holy man farther downstream making elaborate gestures with a stick of incense. Other times he just sat there, looking at the rapids. If it was a sunny day, the flattest rocks would be covered with his laundry: cantaloupe-coloured sarongs, matching handkerchiefs and towels. If he was close enough, I'd smile broadly, place my hands in prayer position, bow slightly, and say, "*Namaste.*" The holy man always seemed amused by this, but he never returned my greeting. Lalita, Phool Chatti's Yoga and Meditation Director, told me he'd taken a twelve-year vow of silence. I'd also been told to avoid contact with him at all costs. But I figured even holy men liked to be smiled at now and again.

I confess that, while he was busy with his incense stick at the river, I took advantage of his absence from the cave and lingered for a few moments at the threshold, looking more closely at the gods and goddesses and his neatly kept fire-pit, until I started to feel guilty and walked quickly back up the hill to the ashram.

I'd overstayed my time at Phool Chatti. A one-week retreat, a sampler of the yogic path, had turned into three. I'd self-tailored the past two weeks to suit my own spiritual needs, which included reading novels, writing poems, and, of course, swimming in the river. Luckily the ashram was slow that time of year, and Lalita was happy as long as I kept quiet. I think she saw me as a lost soul, too fragile to return to the rigours of travelling alone in India. I think she was right.

As the river became colder, Lalita began to talk of closing for the season, so I walked five kilometers into Laxman Jhula and bought a bus ticket to Rajasthan. On impulse I bought the holy man a bag of oranges and left them by the mouth of his cave.

On my last day at the ashram I walked to the Ganges for my final swim. I saw the holy man inside his cave, bent over the fire, snapping twigs. The moment I reached the cave entrance, he turned and gestured for me to enter. I looked nervously back toward the ashram. He slapped the ground, hard, with a twig and fixed me with a scowl. I went inside.

He led me to the altar. There, beneath an image of Shiva, balanced a pyramid of oranges. He pointed to me, to the oranges, to Shiva. He placed his hands in front of his chest in prayer position and bowed his head. Then he rubbed the spine of a cabbage leaf onto the dirt floor and began to write with its juice: *Breakfast. Tomorrow. 7 a.m.* He looked to me for a response. I nodded. He clapped his hands together twice, smiling so widely I could see he had only four teeth. Then he turned his back to me, bent over the fire, and snapped twigs.

When I arrived the next morning, the holy man was stirring a pot over the fire. I offered him the only item I had left in my chocolate stash: a Kit-Kat. He clapped his hands and smiled, gesturing towards a cushion atop a bamboo mat. He busied himself with the pot, and I fidgeted on the cushion, growing more and more nervous, but my nervousness was soon overtaken by curiosity. I was at leisure to examine every detail of the cave: the bedroll, the symbols written in ash on the wall above, the package of incense, the books stacked neatly in a recess. He walked to a shelf made of branches lashed together by twine and extracted an assortment of bags from a large box, then returned to the fire.

Finally the holy man presented me with a mysterious concoction in an ornately patterned copper bowl. He sat in front of me and watched as I took my first spoonful. I'd prepared myself to like it no matter how horrible it tasted. But when it reached my tongue, I raised my eyebrows in surprise, then took another bite, and another. I couldn't stop eating. It was as though he'd captured every flavour I'd ever loved. The sweet, the savoury. It was all there in my copper bowl.

He laughed and gave me more. He pointed to Shiva, to the pot on the fire, to me. He went outside and returned with the spine of a cabbage leaf. *Deva*, he wrote, pointed to me and then to the centre of his forehead. *I see you.* I must have looked confused because he squeezed his eyes shut, opened them, and then wrote: *Good heart. I see you. Inside.*

I panicked for a moment. Could he read my mind? I tried to think pure thoughts, and he laughed. Suddenly his expression changed to one of pain. *Suffer,* he wrote quickly, the cabbage stem beginning to turn to mush. *Too much.*

"I've suffered too much?" I asked, and he nodded.

The holy man clapped his hands and smiled. He threw the cabbage stem aside and picked up a twig. He scratched into the dirt. He pointed to every word. "Good is coming," I said, and he clapped again. "Good is coming," I said, liking the feel of the words in my mouth.

MOTHER GANGES

"ONE DIP IN THE GANGES, and all bad karma, washed away," a taxi driver tells me. And every day, I swim in the Ganges. I walk down the path through the garden, along the small sandy beach, past the tree filled with langur monkeys and to the spot where the Ganges is just a step off a smooth rock. The current is strong here. The rapids very close. I let the river pull me from one rock to the next, until I'm hooked like a dead branch. Then I climb out and lie on a sun-warmed rock gazing up at the Himalayas.

I swim every day, imagining my bad karma sloshing about in the rapids, eddying downstream just before the bridge. I imagine the fish swimming away from it and the ferryboats cutting through its wake. I begin to dress in white and offer a five-armed goddess fresh guavas.

"If you swim every day in the Ganges for one month, never bad body odour again," a yoga instructor tells me. And I swim, every day for a month. My skin becomes smoother, my hair softer. I notice that even on the hottest of days, even when I walk to the village and wait for two hours at the bank to cash a travellers cheque, I don't smell.

"Three deaths offered to Mother Ganges," a holy man tells me. "Death under five, death by cobra bite, death of woman with fetus in belly." And I stand on the smooth rock, trying to read the flow. I step in. Float until I'm hooked.

THE SAINT

THERE WAS A BUZZ IN THE AIR. Devotees dressed in loose white cotton walked briskly, toting clipboards and folding chairs. The staff at the Western Canteen pumped out orders so quickly I barely had time to sit down before my veggie burger arrived. It could have been North America if it weren't for the autorickshaws spewing diesel on the other side of the Amritapuri Ashram walls.

I had my first view of Amma –the Mother of Immortal Bliss, otherwise known as the Hugging Saint – on a billboard. Her doe-like eyes and radiant smile rose above the palm forests of southern India as I entered Amritapuri's maze of flamingo-pink buildings that some called a "utopia in the jungle." High-rise buildings housed a little metropolis of devotees and visitors. A sound system of rock-concert caliber filled the auditorium's stage. Posters advertising astrology readings, kickboxing, and *tabla* lessons competed with the ashram's daily schedule that began at 4:50 a.m. with the chanting of the thousand Names of the Divine Mother.

I took my first bite of veggie burger, enjoying the taste of mustard and dill pickle after months of *dal* and rice. I looked at my table companion – twenty-four-year-old Gabriel from the American Midwest. Gabriel had been here for two months, rarely venturing beyond the ashram walls. His muscular arms were tattooed with Celtic serpents. He closed his eyes while sipping ginger-lemon tea, smiling to himself.

Gabriel leaned back, trying to cross his legs while wearing a long white *lunghi*. "Do you know anything about Mother?" he asked.

"Never heard of her until a few days ago," I confessed.

"Get out! How did you know she'd be here? She's usually on tour right now."

"I didn't know she'd be here."

"Well, it must be destiny then." He sipped his tea. "Like when I met her."

He told me the story of Amma's visit to Kansas City. "People started lining up the night before." He paused to caress a thick silver bracelet around his wrist. "I was skeptical, at first, like you. Until she hugged me."

Gabriel watched as I took another bite of my burger. "She didn't stop hugging. She hugged for nineteen hours straight without taking a break."

Amma was used to hugging; she'd been at it since 1971, and had hugged more than thirty million people, including Sharon Stone, Jim Carrey, Oprah. In a country where gurus were as ubiquitous as *chapatis*, Amma had found her niche. She could have made holy ash flow from the centre of her palm or diamond rings appear out of thin air, but instead she hugged away what she called "the poverty of love."

"I was hooked. I followed her for the rest of the U.S. tour, then sold everything to come here." Gabriel gestured towards the worn dirt path leading into the male-only dormitories. He'd quit his construction job in the States. He'd traded in his tool belt for a silver Amma bracelet. He even had his own personal mantra now. "I just got it a few days ago." He glanced around, lowering his voice: "I was invited to a private meeting with her. She whispered it into my ear."

I sipped my cappuccino, looking at Gabriel, so earnest, so eager to believe.

Gabriel put his hands together in front of his chest in prayer position. "Thank you for sharing your energy with me." He wobbled his head back and forth a little, India-style. "The line-up starts after breakfast, over there." He pointed towards the auditorium.

"Line-up for what?"

"For *darshan* tokens." He stood up, adjusting his *lunghi*. "You need a number if you want a hug."

The next morning, there was even more of a buzz in the air. The dirt pathways of the ashram filled with children in school uniforms, women in saris, men in business suits. A line began to form in front of the thirty-thousand-square-foot Kali Temple, where Amma was scheduled to dole out hugs. I walked through the throngs to the auditorium.

"You're very late," said a woman with a German accent. "You might not get in today." She handed me a plastic red chip painted with a number. "*Darshan* for Indian nationals first," she explained. "Then international visitors."

I rubbed the number on my token as I walked toward the Juice Stall, beginning to feel a little conspicuous. Since I'd been in India, I'd traded in my T-shirts and cargo pants for a collection of colourful *salwar-kameez* and flowy skirts. I'd even painted my toenails. My smiles were met with cold stares from the white-clad westerners.

When the temple doors opened, the crowd became even more animated. Security guards ushered everyone through a security check complete with metal detector. They herded the international visitors upstairs to the viewing gallery, gift shop, thrift store, and travel agency. I walked around the perimeter of the gallery until I had a clear view of the stage. Amma sat on a large throne-like dais, smiling as though we were all her long-lost children, finally reunited. It was difficult not to smile back. A retinue of western and Indian attendants surrounded her. She looked just like the image on the billboard – the kindly, chubby aunt I'd always longed for. She sat cross-legged with the erect posture of a yogi. A woman to her right nodded. The hugs began.

Hours passed and Amma hugged. Between trips to the juice vendor's stall, I watched businessmen collapse in her arms and sob. I watched crying babies silence at her touch. Her smile radiated to the rafters and everyone, including me, began to walk around with goofy looks on their faces. It was difficult to remain cynical in the face of such an unbridled display of emotion, even after I'd entered the gift shop filled with Amma dolls, calendars, fridge magnets, body wash. The contagion of goodwill forced me to consider buying a purse made of recycled Amma curtains – a brocade pattern on heavy, cream-coloured silk – for the price of a week's stay on the ashram.

I read free pamphlets about Amma's empire – a university, hospital, a network of aid organizations recognized by the United Nations. I read that she'd been born in the lotus position and began performing miracles before she could talk. It was said she could turn water to pudding, kiss cobras, divert storms. This all before the hugging began in her parents' cowshed at the age of fourteen. I walked from the gift shop to the Internet station to the thrift store, where used head-to-toe women's swim robes worn in the ashram's outdoor swimming pool were sold, then I returned to the balcony to see how Amma was doing. She was flushed, but barely perspiring in the heat. I wished I could say the same for myself. I'd already taken two cold showers that day and it was only ten o'clock. Between hugs, an attendant squirted what appeared to be perfume onto Amma's bosom. Another fanned her face.

Finally, it was time for the international visitors to queue. I remembered what Gabriel had said about asking Amma for something, either verbally or silently, because she could read minds, of course. The line-up moved quickly. Attendants stood at regular intervals to nudge dawdlers along. I went over a list of possible wishes in my head: World peace. The end of poverty. How about the end of suffering, to cover all bases? Or maybe I should wish to publish a novel? A novel that would change the world? I felt a gentle nudge as I contemplated.

I was almost there. The smell of damp bodies and rose-scented perfume was disorientating. A western attendant asked: "Where are you from?" I had to think for a moment: "Canada." I wondered if I'd been drugged, if someone had slipped something into my freshly squeezed mango juice.

I began to panic when the woman who'd been standing in front of me seconds before staggered out of Amma's arms, crying. I noticed make-up smeared on Amma's pure white sari. I closed my eyes, trying to concentrate on a wish. Peace. End of Suffering. Novel. A hand on my shoulder pushed me down to a semi-kneeling position. Another hand nudged me towards Amma's warm, soft bosom. Amma grasped the back of my neck and pulled me to her breast. She squeezed. Hard. She murmured something that sounded like "Ma, ma, ma, ma." She gave me a small paper bag, which contained, I discovered later, a packet of holy ash and a hard candy. Cherry flavour. My favourite.

Amma gave some sort of secret signal and suddenly I was ushered backstage with the Amma-ites. For some reason, this made me feel euphoric. It even made me forget about what I'd wished for. From backstage I could gaze at the back of Amma's head as she bent and hugged, bent and hugged. It was almost dark by the time she embraced the last international visitor. Her retinue whisked her off through the back door. After ten hours of non-stop hugging, she was still smiling. I walked outside and took deep breaths of dusk.

"Well?" Gabriel asked afterwards at the Western Canteen. "How was it?"

I tried to think of words Gabriel would appreciate. "The energy in the temple was amazing," I said. Gabriel nodded. "I've never experienced anything like it."

"And?"

"It was a great hug." I remembered Amma's strong grip and the smell of roses. I sipped my tea. Gabriel looked at me. Stared, actually.

"Sorry," he said and looked away, then back again.

It was difficult not to return his gaze. His eyes were the same blue as the northern skies of my country.

He giggled. "I'm sorry, I can't stop looking at you. Suddenly I want to know everything about you. Will you go for a coconut with me?"

I noted the shift in his voice, the softness in his eyes. "I can't. Sorry."

"Just one," he whispered. "Later, when it's cooler." He tried to cross his legs and I tried not to look past the raised hem of his *lunghi*.

He reached for my hand, the sort of contact between the sexes discouraged on the ashram. I pulled away. He kept gazing. His irises were flecked with gold.

~

GABRIEL LED ME DOWN a dirt pathway through the palm forests to a wooden bench. "Two, please," he said, signalling the coconut vendor. She swung her machete. She poked straws through the tops of two matching husks.

I wondered if I should tell Gabriel about the wish as he reached for my hand in the darkness and I didn't pull away. Should I tell him that tomorrow morning I planned to leave the ashram, to board the boat that would take me through the backwaters of Kerala and back into the heart of India? From our bench I could see Amritapuri's high-rises, windows ablaze, casting light upon the dark fringe of the palm forest to the shores of the Arabian Sea. Was it so wrong to wish for love? For someone to love you unconditionally?

"Is it sweet?" the coconut vendor asked.

"Yes," I said, and took another sip.

THE ELEPHANT

WE WERE UNITED BY OUR BARE FEET. Those with shoes had left them at the threshold of a 170-foot-high tower adorned with mythical figures, deities, saints, and scholars. A crew of Meenakshi Amman temple workers enforced a "No Shoes Please" sign, and entrepreneurial kids offered to watch footwear for the price of a few pennies. I looked down at my feet, calloused from months of walking upon India in the same pair of flip flops. Streets, alleyways, rice fields, riverbanks. Cow dung, rat poison, monsoon puddle. Now I left my sweaty imprint upon a pathway of marble that felt as soothing as a cold compress.

Inside the temple complex, an elephant stood in a courtyard, her forehead marked with vermillion, ankles adorned with bangles. A young boy positioned a bucket beneath her hindquarters. She urinated. I stood still, mesmerized by the stream, by the sound it made as it hit the bucket. Then I looked up. The elephant's eyes were as large as coconuts, and the look in them was enough to make me want to lead her out into the cardamom forests beyond Madurai, away from those thick stone walls and dim light, from the press of fifteen centuries of worship.

A crowd had gathered by the time the elephant had finished her business. The boy carried the steaming bucket into the bowels of the temple, and the elephant hung her head. As I wandered through the rest of the complex, other elephants tethered to their masters accepted offerings of bananas and garlands of flowers. I hurried past, avoiding that look in their eyes, into the Thousand-Pillared Hall, alongside the dried-up Lake of the Lotus filled with pigeon droppings and picnicking families. As the sun set, streams of worshippers arrived bearing gifts for the deities: cartons of milk, wreaths of hibiscus, packets of potato chips.

I followed a sea of kaleidoscopic saris into the innermost courtyard. Bangles jingled, bells rang. The marble became slick with spilled offerings and sweat. My calloused soles began to vibrate. From a dark corridor, the sound of stomping grew closer and closer.

The crowd followed the procession of elephants around a gold-topped shrine. I circled and circled whatever lay in the centre, on an altar festooned with neon lights, craning my neck above the crowd to glimpse a slender hand of green stone, a lotus. The elephants turned, their footsteps echoing. All at once, the ringing and the clanging stopped, and the crowd changed course, streaming back beneath the tower and into the streets of Madurai.

THE MOURNER

ON THE DAY BEFORE CHRISTMAS I walked towards what my guidebook called the *burning ghats* – Varanasi's main draw, or drawback, depending on how you felt about watching corpses burn. For some reason, I was drawn to the place along the river where smoke blurred the Ganges like a morning mist.

It was almost noon, not the best time to go for a walk along a treeless promenade paved with slabs of stone. Even the polluted waters of the Ganges reflected the searing light of India. Even the crumbling marble of the Maharaja's palace shimmered with heat.

I stopped for a soda water and lime. I stopped for fortune-tellers, boat-*wallahs*, silk merchants, money changers, all touting their services. "No thank-you," I said politely but firmly, careful to look them in the eye so they knew I was serious. But it didn't work. They'd heard it was the Christmas season for us westerners.

"No Merry Christmas gift?" they complained. "No money, no honey!"

I kept walking. I fell into a silent march, determined to be invisible. Passers-by spat red betel nut juice, staining the stone. A row of men pissed along a rampart. Young girls giggled, trailing saris in their wake. Washer-*wallahs* pounded cloth on rock, rhythmic as a tennis match. Wet sheets, waiters' uniforms, a tourist's blue jeans and pink lace bra spread to dry on the sandstone. Prayer bells rang. *Sadhus* chanted. All of India seemed to find their place upon these banks – taking baths, playing cricket, practicing yoga, selling flowers, brushing teeth, rinsing out milk buckets, washing water buffaloes.

The further I walked, the fainter I felt. The breeze shifted, and I caught a whiff of something akin to burnt hair. I turned off the promenade, climbed steep steps, and entered the labyrinthine alleys, hoping it would be cooler.

"People go missing in Varanasi's alleys," the hotel manager at Vishnu Rest House had warned at check-in. He imposed a strict curfew. "The gates lock at 10 p.m. No exceptions." Two of his guests, Japanese girls, had gone missing just last month. In the middle of the day. "I'm not joking," he'd said.

I noted the darkened archways and shuttered windows. Ancient-looking symbols carved into stone. Hidden courtyards overrun by vines. I walked further and further into what felt like the dark heart of the universe.

My guidebook said Varanasi was one of the oldest continually inhabited cities in the world, the "Rome of India." Mark Twain said it was "older than history, older than tradition, older even than legend, and looks twice as old as all of them put together." A bookshop owner told me, "Varanasi is the beating heart of the universe. The secrets of life and death can be discovered here – if you know where to look."

I was lost. The cobbled alleyways narrowed so much I was forced to pat the flank of a cow with sharply curved horns, urging her to move aside. The lane narrowed until temples closed in on both sides: Buddhist, Jain, Hindu. I smelled the chalky dampness of stone, the sharp tang of marigolds, that burning smell again.

Men bearing a home-made stretcher appeared in the alley. Something wrapped in white cloth draped with garlands of flowers bobbed atop the lashed bamboo. The men walked barefoot, chanting. I realized then it was a corpse, wrapped so tightly I saw the outline of its nose.

I followed the cortege until I reached worn stone steps leading to Manikarnika Ghat. Stacks of wood nearly twenty feet high blocked the view of the Ganges. Young boys transported load after load on their heads from boats heaving with logs.

When the stretcher disappeared, another appeared. Then another. And another.

I caught sight of the fires then. Plumes of brownish-black smoke filled the sky. Men wearing dirty T-shirts and *lunghis* managed each blaze. In each group, one man carried a long bamboo pole.

"You shouldn't be standing here," a bare-chested man warned. I apologized and began to walk away as he said, "Come closer for a better view."

He led me through the throngs of workers and mourners. The smoke grew thicker. The stench stronger. He showed me where I could stand. I noticed nick marks on his freshly shaved head.

"That's my father," he said of the corpse atop the pyre. He asked my name. He introduced me to the group of men standing on the platform.

"Canada," they repeated when they learned of my homeland. "A good country," they cooed, becoming more and more animated.

I smiled politely while standing atop the charred ground radiating with heat. A trio of stray dogs on the periphery of the ghat waited patiently. The Ganges flowed slowly past, strewn with flowers. I looked away when they lit the pyre. The fire crackled, and I felt the puff of a breeze laced with heat. It took seconds for the cloth to dissolve in the flames and expose the corpse – the wrinkled skin, the bony thigh. It all burned so quickly. I kept looking away, then back again, lured by the dance of the flames. The man with the bamboo pole poked at the fire. A young boy added more kindling. Something popped in the heat.

"You must stay until his spirit is released to the heavens," the son said, but I wanted to go now. I'd seen enough.

The bamboo pole was passed to the son. He walked to the head of his father's corpse and stood there for a moment, straight-backed, head held high. He raised the bamboo pole above the skull. I turned away. The sound of the crack made me wince. I imagined the soul of his father rising above the smoke. I watched the sky, looking for a sign.

The son returned to my side. I couldn't tell whether tears or sweat ran down his cheek. "Thank you," he said.

The mood became sombre. The men watched the final flickerings of the blaze.

Finally, I walked away, returning to the tomb-like cool of the alleys. I stopped to sit on a wooden bench to drink *chai*, to look at tissue-paper kites rise into the sky. I passed restaurants offering festive meals and live sitar music. I remembered it was Christmas Eve. By the time I found my way back to a familiar twist in the alley, the gate at Vishnu Rest House was locked. I called and called until the owner appeared, asking me where I'd been. I looked towards the sky, to the souls up there that must have been circling Varanasi as surely as the wheeling stars.

THE CITY OF LIGHT

IT'S SUNSET AND I'M DRINKING *chai* at Vishnu Rest House. Milky and sweet. The couple to my left is speaking Japanese, to my right Spanish. We face the Ganges. The Ganga, if you want to sound more Indian. If you want to look more Indian, I'd recommend ditching the jeans and hiking boots. I've opted for a silk fuchsia *salwar-kameez* and a pair of flip-flops. I think that's why I got a better room rate.

It's sunset and the eye-shaped wooden boats are carrying tourists to the cremation *ghats*. It's dark enough to see the fires now. Every time the wind shifts, I can smell the burning flesh. One of the oarsmen told me he rows to the cremation *ghats* when he's depressed. He said, "The sound of bones popping in the heat comforts me."

It's sunset and on the opposite shore the Bollywood film crew is firing up the set lights. They film until late into the night. They've erected bamboo huts and campfire pits. Amidst the huts wander an assortment of holy men – some smeared in ash, some in saffron-coloured sarongs, others in white loincloths. It's difficult to know whether they're real or actors. Except during a dance number.

It's sunset and I'm watching for dolphins. Even though the Ganges is polluted, there are rumours of river dolphins. Yesterday, I thought I saw one, though it could have been a body part. A charred arm? Sometimes at the cremation *ghats*, parts find their way into the river. But this object seemed to do a little jump. I'm sure I saw a splash.

It's sunset and the rooftops are filled with young boys and old men flying kites. Tissue paper. Wooden frames. Thin strings held close to their hearts. Brightly-coloured diamonds jerk their way upwards. Some plummet into *bodhi* tree branches. Others catch an airstream. And then they begin to soar. They soar to the rising moon.

It's sunset and the swallows are flying downriver in swarms. They skim the surface, swallowing mosquitoes. They swoop through the porticos of the Maharaja's palace. They swoop and pirouette and swoop some more. There must be some music playing that they swoop to with such grace. But I can't hear it. On cue, they tilt their wings to the right. Fly directly above our heads. The Japanese, the Spanish and I stop drinking tea. We crane our necks to ogle thousands of ochre-coloured bellies streaming towards the setting sun like iron filings to a magnet. There's a sensation on my skin: a soft, warm puff of air. A tingling. And then they're gone.

THE WAITER

"YOUR HUSBAND WILL BE HAPPY if you're fat." The waiter pointed to my fake wedding ring and extra serving of toast. I brushed a dead fly off the tablecloth.

It was seven in the morning in Kolkata and I was the first guest for breakfast. I'd been up since five and had been waiting for any excuse to escape my room. It was small and stuffy and smelled of mouldy cardboard. Everything was painted the colour of spoiled cream, even the window panes. The cream-coloured air conditioner sounded like a jet engine but I dared not turn it off. When I'd asked for a better room the night before, the front desk agent, who'd been sleeping on the floor before I'd roused him to check in, said, "Ask the breakfast waiter in the morning."

And so I asked. "You are talking pretty, Madame," the waiter said and laughed. He removed the tea cozy and poured me a cup of dishwater-coloured tea. "You are in a very good room, Madame. Much better than Room Fourteen."

An ant climbed out of the marmalade. A slice of fried tomato and two fried mushrooms slid towards the pale eggs. I nibbled a slice of canned pineapple and stuck a spoon in the porridge.

The waiter pointed to a map on the wall, to a state near the Bay of Bengal. "I am from Orissa," he said placing his finger on a well-worn spot. "There is my village. I have a wife and three children."

I'd read of the area, famous for its tigers, mangroves, Irrawaddy dolphins. "How often do you go home?"

"Oh, that is too expensive, Madame. Maybe in another year or two."

"But isn't Orissa just a few hours away?"

"As I said, Madame, very far, and very expensive."

From beyond the dining room, I saw an oasis. Banana trees and potted palms, emerald-coloured parrots flitting from frond to frond. Wicker garden furniture with glass-topped tables. There I could imagine the British Raj sipping gin and tonics with juicy wedges of lime. I was tempted to sit there all day and do the same. But the lounge was closed for renovations, and I had come to Kolkata for something else. This was the "City of Joy" after all; as a teen I'd read of this place once known as Calcutta through the eyes of Dominique Lapierre's slum-dwelling characters. And I knew that when I left this hermetically-sealed hotel and walked onto Sudder Street, I wouldn't have to go far to find it. The child tugging at my sleeve, a baby in her arms, "Madame," she'd say, her curls brittle with dust. "We are so hungry, Madame." The woman sitting on her haunches by the side of the road, rocking back and forth, shreds of clothing hung to dry with a piece of twine. The boy pulling a wooden rickshaw, straining at the waist, rubber flip flops slapping the pavement.

How to leave one world and enter the other? How to enter the largest democracy in the world, where the highest number of undernourished people on Earth live? Where hundreds of millions live on less than two dollars a day? I buy a cup of *chai* for twelve cents, lunch for a dollar. I ride the Metro for a dime. I cash a travellers cheque for one hundred American dollars, leaving the bank with such a large wad of bills crammed into my money belt that I look pregnant. Is this what it feels like to be rich? This secret thrill of knowing I could buy almost anything I want right now? I could stay in the best hotel in the city, eat at the best restaurant. I could buy hand-woven silks and a cartload of jasmine flowers. I could buy it all and you would still be crouched there, by the side of the road, watching the buses pass.

I had come to Kolkata to help. Instead I could barely function. The heat exhausted me. The heartbreak of millions overwhelmed me. I knew I was a liability everywhere I went, in need of clean water, uncontaminated food, a toilet. So I sought out Kolkata's famous coffee houses and bookstores. I walked through neighbourhoods where mansions stood behind barbed wire fences and armed guards, where women with pure gold woven through their saris talked on cell phones and ate croissants in European-style bistros.

The waiter cleared away my half-eaten breakfast. "Your husband will not be happy, Madame."

THE LONELY GIRL

They unfurled from a dark mass into gossamer wisps, passing through the deodar cedars like ghosts, twisting along footpaths through the tea plantations, revealing entire villages in their wake: rusty tin roofs, white-washed walls. The clouds seeped through my French windows, settling on a four-poster teak bed that had originally belonged to G.H. Batterbury, Chief Engineer of the Darjeeling Himalayan Railway in the early 1900s. I shivered.

I stood on the balcony listening to the cluck of chickens, the laughter of children, the chatter of women sorting grain. They never looked my way, but I knew they could see me up here, alone, looking down and out towards the tea plantations, and across the foothills towards Darjeeling. They could see the ornate latticework of the balcony, the ochre-coloured walls of Kurseong's Cochrane Place, the restored colonial home of Percy John Cochrane, MBE. They must have known how much I'd paid to stay in the room named after a Himalayan peak – The Pandim – the attendant of the god of the mountain.

The prayer flags began to flap. And I stood there, looking down, looking out.

"Are you travelling lonely?" was a question I had been asked often since I landed in Delhi. Now as the monsoon winds rattled the doors of Cochrane Place's empty rooms, I wondered if it was true. Before India, alone had meant a desire to look inwards, to experience the world without the input of others, to test one's mettle and resourcefulness, to strengthen one's inner core. But here, alone had become synonymous with lonely.

The heaviest object in my backpack was a guidebook called The Lonely Planet. It had the size and heft of a bible and was as essential to my survival as the ark must have been to Noah.

I asked myself, Am I lonely? Yes. I was alone to face the stares, the curiosity that led to questions such as, "What are those on your arms?"

"Freckles."

"Oh, I am so sorry," said a woman on the train, adjusting her *dupatta*. "My sister also has a skin condition."

For years I'd travelled as an observer. In India I noticed straw brooms, *ghee* tins planted with marigolds, crimson saris, plastic sandals, acrylic cardigans.

But in India a blonde Caucasian woman was more the observed than the observer. Gone was my romantic image of the lone traveller quietly taking notes. "What are you writing? Are you a writer?" asked a man at the *chai* stand.

"I'm writing about your country," I answered.

"Have you ever meditated?"

"No."

"You will never write anything of worth unless you learn how to meditate."

Being observed took some getting used to. The locals seemed able to gauge my mood the moment I stepped out the door of my hotel. They seemed to know when I was feeling vulnerable, or when I became a bliss bunny – a westerner high on borrowed Indian spirituality. Like the time I'd left Phool Chatti Ashram all full of peace and love, thinking only good was coming, and that all my bad karma had floated downstream. But on the night bus to Rajasthan, it hadn't taken long for all that peace and love to dissipate. Five minutes of the guy beside me craning his head to read along was all it took to slam my book closed and turn towards the window.

"What's your name?" he asked. "Where are you from?"

Silence.

Two friends sitting in front turned around. They mimicked my every move. When I finally closed my eyes to feign sleep, they laughed.

"What's your name?" the man asked, touching my arm.

"Don't touch me!" I hissed with all the venom I could muster. I was ready to kill.

"Ohhhh," said one of the friends. "Look how angry."

The bus turned onto Grand Trunk Road, bound for Delhi. The driver dimmed the lights. The trio of friends began taking swigs from a plastic water bottle. The smell of alcohol was so strong my nostrils tingled.

"What's your name?" the man poked my shoulder. "Where are you from?"

The more they drank, the more afraid I felt. I scanned the bus for allies. My fellow passengers were fast asleep. When I'd finally worked up the courage to ask the bus driver for help, the trio passed the bottle to him. He drank.

Another seventeen hours to Rajasthan. I'd heard about this kind of harassment in India, called "Eve teasing." I knew it was punishable by law. I'd witnessed Indian women tell these kinds of men off with a few choice words I wished they'd teach me.

"What's your name?" the man touched my thigh. "I just want to be your friend."

"Stop it!" I yelled and slapped his hand away.

"Where are you from?"

We jolted to a stop. The bus driver flicked on the interior lights, rousing the passengers. Sirens sounded in the distance. An accident up ahead. I used the distraction to ask the man across the aisle if I could switch seats with him. His wife patted my hand, shaking her head at the three drunk men. I admired her golden bangles and diamond nose piercing. Yes, she was from Rajasthan. Sorry, she didn't speak much English.

Am I lonely? Yes. I put on a brave face. I read books and wrote in journals. I studied the *Lonely Planet* before every excursion, memorizing routes so I could walk like I knew where I was going. But when I walked into the village of Kurseong with the eyes of everyone from the school girl to the jeep driver to the fruit vendor upon me, each one of them thinking Is she alone?, my footsteps echoed throughout the Himalayas: Alone, Alone, Alone.

I walked into a shop and ordered a 7-Up. "Just one?" the storekeeper asked. She smiled kindly. "Where are you from?" She opened the cap and stuck a straw in the bottle. I drank, hidden from view, observing share-jeeps laden with boxes and passengers, bound for the plains of Siliguri. Goats ate from a pile of garbage. A crowd of protesters marched past, carrying rolled-up mattresses and blankets.

"Those are the hunger strikers," the shopkeeper said. "Striking for Gorkhaland in the tradition of Gandhi."

It was time to head back out onto Pankhabari Road. I waited for the street to clear, took a deep breath. "Thank you," I said.

"*Dhanyavaad,*" she said, bowing her head.

Layers of dark clouds swooped across the hills, masking the view of the foothills within seconds. The fruit vendor brought in his crates. Tea workers ran for shelter with baskets bobbing on their heads. Rain fell in curtains. Alone, Alone, Alone, my sneakers squished. Rain streaked down my face. I tasted the salt of my sweat, the grime of the road. Ahead, the protesters huddled beneath the shell of an unfinished cinder block house, clutching their blankets to their chests.

Suddenly, the rain seemed to stop. I looked beside me and there stood a man in a white *lunghi*, umbrella held aloft, one shoulder exposed to the rain. He led me towards the shelter. The protesters cheered and clapped as we drew closer. "Come here!" they called to us. "Come!"

YOU, BESIDE ME

THEY THINK I'M HERE TO SEE the Taj Mahal, but I'm here to see you, in the second-class compartment, offering stories then *parathas* then your address in Mumbai. You, in the frayed cardigan on the public bus paying my fare, then disappearing into the fruit market. You, crouched on the pavement dying cloth or hemming trousers or fixing the strap on my sandal. You, who cannot read or write, yet speak my language and the language of your village, and of your cousin's village. You, asleep on the floor of Varanasi station, thin blanket wrapped around your son. You, who gave me a silk scarf the colour of forget-me-nots. You, stirring *chai* in your stone hut. You, beside me during the monsoon, umbrella held aloft, shielding me from the rain.

THE HOTEL OWNER

THE GREENHOUSE WAS FILLED with chrysanthemums, but Rita was looking for something else. She spoke in hushed tones. The owner looked uncertain for a moment, then returned with what looked like a chunk of bark. Rita shook her head. He returned with a bigger chunk covered with tufts of moss. Rita smiled. She asked for more "exactly like these," she said. With a bow, the owner disappeared.

He quoted a price and seemed surprised when Rita opened her purse and handed him the money. "It was a good deal," she explained afterwards. "Besides, what he sold me is rare. Some might say illegal."

Rita planned to carry the secret ingredient for her orchid collection – a growing medium harvested from the ecologically rich Darjeeling Hills, where nearly 300 species of wild orchids thrived – on tonight's train to Kolkata.

"What if someone stops you?" I asked.

"I'm travelling First Class," she said.

There were other errands to complete in Kurseong before she boarded the train. She signalled the driver of the Cochrane Place's Land Rover to continue. We wound down the mountain past unfinished cinder block houses where bed sheets hung on lines strung between rebar rods, where sisters washed one another's hair in the afternoon light, and passionfruit vines hung from the terraces.

Rita tapped the back of the driver's seat when it was time to stop again. He jumped to open his boss's door and escorted us into a building that looked recently bombed. I held my breath until the stench of urine subsided. But Rita remained unfazed. She may have been petite, grey-haired, and wearing the khaki-coloured trousers and sneakers of a common tourist, but Rita was nothing short of regal. She was as sophisticated a Kolkatan as they came, living in a house filled with art and flowers, golfing at the Royal Calcutta Golf Club, wearing hand-embroidered saris. "My husband is a scientist," she had told me earlier. "He weaves thread from platinum." Rita's family had acquired Cochrane Place as a getaway from the Kolkatan summer, recently transforming the building into a boutique hotel – "restored in stone, log & cast-iron splendour," their website promised.

The driver awakened the owner of a shop filled with statues of the Buddha and gestured to Rita.

"My son is hosting a party for his colleagues in Singapore and I thought he'd like to decorate with Tibetan prayer flags," she said. "They always look so festive."

The shop owner scurried about laying all manner of flag on the counter. I noticed the ones popular back home, at places with names like Tibet Shoppe or *Shanti* Baba, stores filled with incense and brass Buddhas. Rita brushed these cheap cotton versions aside.

"The silk ones," she said.

When the shop owner realized Rita was planning to buy a significant quantity of his best prayer flags, his eyes lit up. Rita examined his wares, rubbing the edges of flags between her fingers. "Real silk," she said.

The shop owner rummaged beneath his cash box and laid stacks of bright flags on the counter. Rita nodded. She extracted a small golden pencil and notepad from her purse and wrote down a price. The owner crossed it out and wrote down a different price. This continued until Rita placed several crisp bills on the counter. The owner nodded.

"Now, just the fabric to make covers for the water bottles," she said, instructing the driver to head to the market. "Unless you find all this dreary."

"Of course not," I said as we drove down the steep hill surrounded by stalls hanging with aluminum pots and pans, towel sets, plastic buckets.

When we returned to Cochrane Place, Rita invited me for dinner later that evening. I settled back into The Pandim, watching from the balcony as the monsoon clouds rose from the base of the valley, listening as the rain obliterated all other sound. The storm ended as quickly it began. Pines dripped. Pigeons cooed. Sunlight striped the hills section-by-section, each white house a sliver of brightness. The women emerged from the village below, baskets on their heads. Young boys spread mats to play cards in the fading light. The earth steamed.

At dinner, I could tell Rita was worried about leaving on the 10:30 train that night. There were threats of a *bandh* (strike) and violence. Local businesses had been encouraged to "contribute" to the cause of the Gorkhaland movement for an independent state, I'd been told. But

I had no idea if Cochrane Place had complied. In the past, refusals had resulted in a few broken windows, but nothing more. I thought of the night when I'd woken to what sounded like gunshot in the village below. I'd stood on the balcony as house lights turned on, as the villagers yelled words I couldn't understand, as doors slammed, and cars screeched to a halt. Cochrane Place had gone dark as the night watchman paced back and forth on the terrace.

"Just the monsoon," the concierge had told me in the morning, and I'd wondered if I'd dreamed it all.

But Rita didn't want to talk about politics during dinner. Politics weren't conducive to the enjoyment of the betel-leaf *pakoras* served by an elderly waiter, the bite-sized samosas. She wanted to talk about art and books, her favourite travel writers. "You must read Pico Iyer," she said.

The waiter's hand shook as he refilled our water, spilling a few drops on Rita's lap. His face reddened. "I am so sorry, Madame. I am so sorry."

"It's fine. Do not worry." Rita patted his arm. "He is nervous to be serving me," she said as he returned to the kitchen. "He has never done this kind of work before. Most people here have only ever worked in the tea fields."

I'd seen those workers, blue tarps tied to their waists, stooped over seas of green leaves. I'd seen them walking barefoot through the streets, heavy loads tied to foreheads with tumplines, focusing on the ground beneath them, never looking up.

The waiter, like most of the staff at Cochrane Place, came from one of the poor villages surrounding Kurseong. Rita said she'd been to their homes, met their families. "I think that's the best way to interview someone," she said.

The chef served multi-layer pilau decorated with glowing green pepper lanterns. I became self-conscious the more Rita talked about what sounded like an opulent life in Kolkata. Was I using the right fork? Was my posture straight enough? Should I tell Rita that she was dining with a backpacker who didn't usually stay in places described as "boutique hotels," that no one would read the book I was planning to write, that she'd wasted her day escorting me around in her Land Rover, pointing out the lemon pines and the mango pines and the small white orchids Kurseong was named for? But I suspected Rita knew all this; she listened intently and looked me in the eye. I was the only one who cared about such matters.

Outside the dining room windows, villages invisible by day began to dot the dark slopes of the Himalayas with specks of light. Soon Rita was telling me she wasn't really from India.

"I grew up in what's now Pakistan, in Lahore," she said. "We were forced to leave during Partition." She told me about her grandfather, a surgeon, shot in his car. Her father, also a surgeon, shot in the hospital he had founded. The rest of her family hid for three days under a hospital bed ("they knew us there, so let us in," she said), eating a boiled egg a day until it was safe to leave the newly formed country. Train after train arrived in Lahore, all of its Pakistan-bound passengers slaughtered. Train after train left Lahore, all of its India-bound passengers slaughtered on the other side of the new border. Rita's family fled on foot to a refugee camp in Madhya Pradesh. "We lost everything material," she said. "But we were alive. My story is the story of millions."

Rita poured me a cup of tea. "No," she said gently as I reached for milk and sugar. "Not with Darjeeling." The tea master stood by, awaiting her approval. She sipped and nodded. He returned to his station flanked by a collection of teapots and tins, an armoire of teacups. Framed quotations decorated the walls: "Where there's tea, there's hope"; "Tea is drunk to forget the din of the world."

More and more villages lit up the dark slopes. The chef served a steamed banana pudding with passionfruit sauce.

"Your company has been delightful," Rita said as she rose to prepare for the Darjeeling Mail. "Please visit me in Kolkata someday."

I stood with the staff in the courtyard to bid her farewell, watching the Land Rover's tail lights zigzag down the terraced tea fields, and into the plains of Siliguri.

THE JESUIT PRIEST

You probably don't remember me. We met in the sitting room of Cochrane Place – *pakoras*, large bottles of Black Label lager. I laughed when you took a swig. You said, "Weren't expecting that, were you?" No, I wasn't. The only Jesuits I'd ever seen had starred in films set in jungles, building chapels and dug-outs. But then there you were – in the foothills of the Himalayas, where monsoon clouds steeped in tea fields and passed through the pines like ghosts. I wanted to see the peaks of Khangchendzonga. You wanted to visit a little boy whose mother had just died of typhus, but you weren't feeling well that day. You spoke as though the world were as black and white as your *biretta* and cassock, and maybe it was in a country where you were either hungry or not, homeless or not, alone or not. When I asked how best to help you answered: "Just be there." And I should have listened. Be there to hold a hand. Be there to shiver in the cold and sweat in the heat. Be there to get your hands dirty and your heart broken.

THE ACUPUNCTURISTS

IT WAS JUST AFTER TEN in the morning when the power went out. But Darpan was prepared. He switched on his headlamp, beaming light onto my left ear. "Inhale, please," he said, positioning a needle above the acupuncture point *Shen Men*. "Exhale, please." He pricked the skin. I winced for a split second, then relaxed; I was in good hands. Darpan was no stranger to needles. For fifteen years he'd used them to inject low-grade heroin into his veins. But now the only needles he used were fine-tipped and sterile, aimed towards strategic points on the outer ear. "Good job," Dr. Laura Louie said when Darpan completed "needling" the first point on my ear – a pathway now unblocked by the needle's fine tip, allowing *Qi* – the Chinese term for life energy – to flow freely again.

It was the beginning of week two – the second and final week of Acupuncture Detox Specialist (ADS) training at Kurseong's Red Cross. Outside on Pankhabari Road, groups of tea pickers hurried past. Overloaded share jeeps careened downhill, honking at anything that crossed their path. But nothing distracted Darpan and the three other ADS trainees – all male, all ex-addicts – from the surface of my outer ear.

Hand-picked by Kalyan – a harm-reduction network formed to educate communities about the risks of injection drug use – the trainees had travelled to Kurseong from towns in the Himalayan foothills known more for premium tea gardens and alpine trekking than drug addiction. They had come to do what had never been done before in these parts – to talk about clean needles and abscess management, condoms, and collapsing veins. They'd come to learn a three-thousand-year-old Chinese medical practice and apply it to one of this region's most modern tragedies – soaring rates of injection drug use and HIV/AIDS. Rates which had caused India's National Institute of Cholera and Enteric Diseases to declare an epidemic requiring urgent intervention on local, national, and international levels.

But interventions had been slow to trickle into these hills. So slow that the addicts themselves took matters into their own hands. And it was a lone doctor from Canada – trained in acupuncture and naturopathy – who had volunteered to help them.

Dr. Louie adjusted her headlamp. "A little too far to the left," she advised Darpan, and inserted a new needle into my ear. The other trainees gathered around, casting beams of light across the Red Cross, taking note.

The *Lonely Planet* warned to expect the unexpected of this country. I didn't expect to meet Dr. Louie while drinking Darjeeling in the dining room of Cochrane Place. Nor did I expect her to invite me to the Red Cross to meet a group of ex-addicts training in the National Acupuncture Detoxification Association protocol, a widely recognized therapy where five needles are inserted into standardized spots on each ear to reduce withdrawal symptoms associated with substance abuse.

Anyone who has met Dr. Louie would tell you she's impossible to refuse. She made me want to put down my cup of tea and help. She made me want to wear long, swishy skirts and necklaces weighted by chunks of art. She made me want to fly to India with thousands of acupuncture needles to donate stashed in my luggage and just walk through the Nothing to Declare door, smiling.

She made me say things like "You can practice on me," to four overly eager trainees whom Dr. Louie must remind to dispose of used needles, and to always, *always* unwrap new ones.

"We have plenty of needles," she constantly reassured them.

Darpan adjusted his headlamp. "Inhale, please," he said, positioning a fresh needle above *Sympathetic*. "Exhale, please." He pricked my skin. I tried not to wince. Even though I wanted to help, I was terrified of needles. But Darpan's touch was gentle, his voice soothing. I focused on his T-shirt embroidered with a Chinese dragon, then on his face, as he searched for the next point on my ear. I wondered if his six-year-old son, the son he'd told me he isn't permitted to see anymore, had the same chubby cheeks, the same Buddha-like smile. "Inhale, please," he said and I took a deep breath.

I thought of what Darpan told me earlier about hitting rock bottom during the last days of his addiction. "I couldn't die. I couldn't live," he'd said of the dilemma of wanting to kill himself but knowing even that was impossible. Buddhists can't die – they are reborn again and again, in realms with names like cold hell, hot hell, hungry ghost hell. "It was better to live," he explained.

"Exhale, please." The needle pricked *Kidney*. I focused on the other trainees – on Prabin's *Italia* jersey, on Karma's Converse sneakers, on Sanjay's button-down shirt so neatly tucked in. Though they bore crude-looking tattoos of Batman symbol and cannabis leaf, there were no track marks or hollowed-out eyes. I knew they were over thirty, but they barely seemed to have aged past eighteen. They looked more like hip IT graduates than men who had spent half their lives injecting drugs into their veins.

"Good job," Dr. Louie said when Darpan completed all five points on my ear. "You don't have to be suffering from withdrawal symptoms to benefit." Finally, I began to relax. Everyone switched off their headlamps, conserving batteries. Who knew when the power would come back on?

Even with power, the light was dim at Kurseong's Red Cross. A single bulb dangled, interrogation-style, from the ceiling. But maybe it was better we couldn't see too well. The colonial-style bungalow – one of the town's many reminders of the British Raj, who had once sought refuge here from the Kolkatan heat – had seen better days. Hardwood floors were worn bare. The fireplace, complete with bevelled mantelpiece, functioned as a garbage can. In the back of the house, where "Ladies" was scrawled in white chalk on a plywood door, I turned on the faucet, hoping what Dr. Louie had told me earlier was just a joke. But it wasn't. There was no running water.

But such conditions failed to daunt Dr. Louie and her trainees. They donned headlamps. They squirted disinfectant onto their hands with religious fervour. Sanjay cleaned the surface of the worktable with rubbing alcohol. Prabin arranged six red plastic lawn chairs around the perimeter of the living room. Karma laid out new acupuncture needles on a square of paper towel. Darpan opened a plastic candy jar labeled "Used Needles."

Dr. Louie explained the mission of the day in English. Only when they were certain Dr. Louie – Dr. Laura, as they called her – had finished speaking, did the Nepali translations begin. Today they would practice acupuncture on volunteers from the community. They would take turns. They shouldn't feel shy. Dr. Laura would observe and help them. Now they just had to wait.

They didn't have to wait long. Soon, several women in rainbow-hued saris were waiting at the door. Word was out that free treatments were being offered at the Red Cross. It didn't matter that no one had heard of acupuncture before.

The women were shy in front of the male trainees, lowering their eyes. But when they saw me leaning against the wall, notebook in hand, they placed their hands in prayer position. They bowed their heads. "*Namaste,*" they said and smiled. One by one, they offered me their lawn chairs, until the trainees explained they'd need them for their treatment. They settled then – eyes darting back to my face every few minutes.

While the trainees distributed consent forms, the chants of "Gorkhaland! Gorkhaland!" rose up from Pankhabari Road. Every day the protesters marched and every day I felt a little more nervous. I'd read of this region's massive unemployment, illiteracy, poverty. I'd read of refugees and migrant workers, unstable borders, and militant groups. The threat of violence loomed as menacingly as the monsoon clouds. But Sanjay said, "Drugs are more dangerous than terrorists."

The monsoon swept through the street, sending rubbish flying and rain clattering on the tin roof. Yet the feeling was tranquil inside the living room of the Red Cross. Karma bent beside the woman in a red sari, reading her consent form aloud, pointing to where she could sign her name with an X. Prabin tried to steady his hand, shaking, I was told, after years of injecting spasmoproxyvon – an over-the-counter muscle relaxant usually prescribed for menstrual cramps. "Inhale, please," he said to the woman whose cheeks were whittled to bone. Darpan helped an elderly man step across the threshold, listening to his complaints of a sore knee. A teen-aged boy arrived, thin and nervous, and Sanjay took his arm, guiding him into a more private room.

The volunteer patients closed their eyes. Needles sprouted from their ears like silver whiskers. Occasionally, the women caught sight of one another and giggled. They'd been instructed to relax, sleep if they'd like, for forty-five minutes, while the treatment took effect.

Meanwhile the trainees tidied their work-site. Their relief was palpable. They had worried no one would come. They had worried they wouldn't get a chance to practice their new skills. They had told me this was the first time they'd done something they were proud of, something that helped to forget about the stigma of being an ex-addict and possible carrier of HIV.

As the rains died down, the chanting of "*Gorkhaland! Gorkhaland!*" resumed. The women in saris began to stir. It was time to remove their needles. With expert precision, the trainees extracted them one by one, careful to deposit them in the plastic candy jar. The sound of a Hindi pop song broke their concentration. Karma fished around the folds of the elderly gentleman's tunic and extracted a cell phone. "Tell her I'll be home soon," the gentleman said.

Quietly, the women in saris took their leave, entering Pankhabari Road with umbrellas held aloft. They caught my eye one last time and bowed their heads, saying, "*Dhanyavaad.*"

In the doorway, the elderly gentleman leaned on his cane. "Can I come back tomorrow?" he asked.

THE ORCHID GROWER

THE MOON WAS ALMOST FULL. Mr. Pempahishey sat in Holumba Haven's courtyard in a well-worn T-shirt and a pair of drawstring shorts. It was only when I got closer that I noticed the rifle leaning against his knee. I tried to get past with a nod or a good evening, but Mr. Pempahishey was in the mood to chat. "Why, you're a busy young lady," he said when he noticed my haste. He looked up at the moon, his hair the same colour as its pale yellow orb.

I tried not to look at the rifle. It glinted in the moonlight as though just polished. Mr. Pempahishey looked at the rifle too, smiling as he patted its barrel. "Oh, such a pleasant evening," he said. "The stars are so much brighter this time of year."

The moon rose high above the orchidaria where his seedlings lay in wait. Thousands of orchids – Indo-Burmese, Himalayan, exotic. He oversaw their nurturing just as he oversaw everything else at Holumba Haven – the guest huts, the partridges, the caged rabbits, the wild turkeys, the guinea pigs, the guard dog. "For your safety," warned a sign on the door of my guest cottage, "please remain indoors between 10 p.m. and 6 a.m. when the guard dog is released."

Holumba Haven was Mr. Pempahishey's self-built kingdom and he did what he pleased there. I knew it would be impolite to ask about the rifle.

"Yes, a very pleasant evening," I said, breathing in the scent of the gardens – the jacaranda, hibiscus, the delicate feathery pines – and trying to forget about the chaos of Kalimpong beyond the gates. Today the walk into town along Hill Cart Road had been even more trying than usual. I didn't know it was a festival day. Flatbed trucks carrying *papier-mâché* effigies of ten-armed goddesses to be submerged in the Teesta River had clogged the narrow road. Every truck had hosted its own mini-party complete with fireworks, drumming, boom boxes, chanting.

"Go back to America!" a group of teenage boys had yelled from behind a goddess's writhing torso.

"Yes, a beautiful night," I answered Mr. Pempahishey. I stood there for a few moments admiring the moon. "Well, it's almost ten o'clock," I said.

"Did my son show you the orchids yet?"

"Yes, Norden showed me this morning."

Mr. Pempahishey reached behind to pick a hibiscus blossom, twirling its stem between his fingers. "Only one orchid is blooming right now," he said. "The *Vanda cristata*. You should have come during a different season to view the orchids." He picked up the rifle. "Well, it's ten o'clock."

~

"THE HIMALAYAS!" NORDEN HAD YELLED at six o'clock that morning, knocking on my door as though the mountain range was an invading army. "The Himalayas!"

I'd splashed cold water on my face and walked to the ridge at the top of the two-acre property where the pines cleared and you could see across the valley.

"It's the first time they've appeared since the beginning of the monsoon," Norden said. "Just wait a moment, the clouds will clear again."

And they did. The peaks lit up one by one. Massive, snow-clad peaks that shrank the world to minutiae.

"Look at that 'V' shape." Norden pointed. "That's the pass to Lhasa. The Old Silk Road. It's not very far away but none of us can go there now. Politics have changed everything."

"What politics?" I asked. The disputed Chinese/Indian border, the Gorkhaland movement, the Maoists?

The Pempahisheys, I'd learned, loved to talk. They even offered subject discussions upon request. Subjects ranged from botany to geography to history. They specialized in Tibetan cultural history and religion in the trans-Himalayan region. But there was no need to arrange a discussion. Every morning at breakfast the stories began. I'd learned about the characteristics of migrant workers, the traditional dress of the Bhutanese royalty, the article Mr. Pempahishey had written, "Orchid Eaters of Shangri-La," published in the *American Orchid Society Bulletin* of 1974.

"Have you ever heard of Dr. Graham?" Norden asked as he set down my porridge. "Dr. Graham was a missionary from Scotland. He founded a boarding school in Kalimpong. And not just a school – there's a workshop, farm, bakery, swimming pool, hospital. My father went there for a time. That's why he's so fond of wearing shorts. That was part of their uniform, you see."

I'd noticed Mr. Pempahishey's penchant for wearing shorts regardless of temperature and the fact I'd yet to see any other Indian man wearing shorts. I buttered my toast, smiling at the sunflower placemats.

After breakfast I watched Thinlay, Norden's wife, fill copper bowls at the free-flowing spring, elegant as a Tibetan princess, hair swinging in the sunlight, while the children played by a pond filled with lotuses. Every morning my head swirled with stories.

"You want to write about India, don't you?" Norden asked as I sat down to dinner. He was there the instant I sat down at the checkered tablecloth. There must have been a motion sensor to alert him the moment I crossed the threshold of the dining room. I knew they worried that I was lonely. Should I tell them I didn't mind eating alone as I read my book or admired the antiques filling the wooden armoire and hanging on the walls? The horse bridle. Tribal masks. Heavy strands of Tibetan coral and turquoise beads.

Norden ladled a spoonful of Sikkimese rice onto my plastic plate, part of a matching set that included everything from the saltshakers to the butter dish to the marmalade pot. "Someone called Kiran Desai wrote a book set in Kalimpong – *The Inheritance of Loss*. Have you heard of it?"

Yes, I'd heard of the Man Booker Prize-winning novel and had read it twice.

"Some people don't like that book in this town," Norden said. "A writer shouldn't call the truth fiction when so many people die."

It was time for the *momos*. Tonight they were stuffed with lotus root and Kalimpong cheese. "How is everything?" Thinlay asked as she set the plate down.

"Wonderful, thank you," I said, wishing she'd join us. But I knew it was Norden's job to entertain the guests. He put his hands in his pockets and looked towards Hill Cart Road.

"You'd never know that just twenty years ago severed heads hung in net bags from poles on the road below," he said.

The dining room was empty. The Japanese banker from Mumbai was on a tour of Dr. Graham's. The journalist from London was playing golf.

"Whose heads were they?" I asked, putting down my fork.

"School headmasters. A reporter. People accused of being informers. Many were killed in infighting between splinter groups seeking an independent state. We heard stories of brutal slaughter and even cannibalism."

"Did you know anyone who was killed?"

"I still know people who are killed." Norden scooped more rice onto my plate. "Kiran Desai calls an incident that happened on July 27, 1986, fiction. Thirteen people were registered as dead that day." He gestured to the empty chair across from me. "May I?" He sat down for the first time since I'd arrived nearly a week ago.

"It was the day of a protest," he began. "The Central Reserve Police Force and the State Armed Police Forces tried to quell the movement and threw tear gas. But the wind was blowing in the wrong direction. The tear gas blew back in their faces. The protesters became bold and ran after the police. That's when I heard the shooting."

The cook arrived with a plastic casserole dish. Norden lifted the lid. "*Dal Makhani*. Your friend Dr. Laura loves this dish." He scooped some onto my plate. "Now, where was I?"

"The shooting."

"Oh, yes. I ran down to the road. There were bodies everywhere. The wounded were hiding in culverts. I ran to get my father. 'We need to get the jeep out of the garage!' I yelled. My dad drove with the wounded in his arms. There was blood everywhere." He fiddled with the salt shaker. "My dad kept driving until we reached a checkpoint," he continued. "A policeman held a gun to my head. My father started shouting: 'Don't shoot! He's my son! My son!' The policeman must have recognized him – my grandfather used to be the local chief of police – and let us go."

The cook set another platter on the table. "Manchurian Veg," Norden said.

"That's okay," I said as he reached for the ladle. "I've had enough."

He looked around, making sure we were still alone. I could hear his children playing outside by the lotus pond. I could hear Mr. Pempahishey directing the gardeners in the orchidarium on the slope above the dining room.

Norden fiddled with the ladle of the Manchurian Veg. "Suddenly a little boy in the street recognized one of his friends inside our jeep.

'Stop!' he yelled. 'That's my friend!' I tried to explain the jeep was full, that there was simply no room – but the boy tried to jump in and be with his friend. I asked him to leave, and when he got out and was running away, I heard a shot. The policeman shot that little boy in the back."

Thinlay arrived to take away my plate. "The cook is making you a special dessert," she said. She walked back into the kitchen, balancing platters on her arms.

"Our jeep did many trips that day. One man and one woman literally died in my arms," Norden said, wiping a crumb from the checkered tablecloth. "But the worst part of the story is that I can still see that little boy, especially when I look at my son. I can still hear his voice."

THE COOK

"SIKKIM HIMALAYAN ACADEMY?" I asked at the bus stand in Bhuriakhop, a small village in West Sikkim. A girl wearing a school uniform of blue skirt and white blouse beckoned me aboard a minibus packed with elementary school students.

"Here," the girl said about ten minutes later in front of a small clearing in the forest. A woman wearing the burgundy robe of a Tibetan nun appeared. "Uncle!" she called.

Uncle crouched in a dark corner of the kitchen shack, scrubbing a giant pot with a scrap of cloth. "You will be staying with Uncle while you're here," Hedwig, the wearer of the burgundy nun's habit and one of the directors of Sikkim Himalayan Academy, said. "That way you will benefit culturally and the community will benefit financially." Her Dutch accent was as crisp and fresh as a tulip. "But don't worry, it won't be more than ten dollars."

"A day?" I asked.

"A week. If we give them too much, it can create problems."

Uncle put down the pot and swung my backpack onto his shoulders. The three of us walked through the grounds of Sikkim Himalayan Academy – a residential school founded in 2003 by two local teachers plus Hedwig and another Dutch volunteer to provide "education and living opportunities to underprivileged children from remote areas of Sikkim." Thirty students called this place home. I heard their voices reciting the alphabet in English as we walked past the open window of a classroom. We passed the outdoor toilets and shower stalls until we reached a steep brick-lined path leading straight into the clouds.

"I call this the yellow-brick road," Hedwig laughed. She told me paths such as these existed all over Sikkim, cutting swaths through the rainforest and into the most remote villages. "A government initiative," she said. "Careful of the leeches. It's that time of year."

Leeches loved the rainy season, Hedwig said, and didn't confine themselves to water around here. "Never take a shortcut." She pointed beyond the path to where vine and leaf and grass and flower literally dripped with life.

Uncle forged ahead despite the weight of my backpack. Hedwig followed close behind. They stopped every once in a while to wait for me. We passed garden plots flush with squash, corn, peas, onions. Cosmos and marigolds lined the path to every white-washed hut. Beneath shelters made of woven palm fronds, cows and goats ate from wooden troughs. After one last steep incline, we reached Uncle's home, three single-storey rooms built of cinder block, their separate doors facing the mountains.

"That's the water spigot," Hedwig said. "Where you can fill buckets for the shower."

"And where should I take a shower?"

Hedwig pointed to a flat-roofed shed with two wooden doors. "Pit toilet on the left, shower on the right."

Uncle led us along the veranda and into a freshly mopped room decorated with posters. One featured a baby sitting in a wicker chair holding balloons: "Discover Happiness in Things Around You." Another, a bouquet of roses: "Nature are witnesses to your thoughts and deeds."

"This is Uncle's first time hosting a volunteer," Hedwig said.

Uncle looked at Hedwig and spoke. "He says you are very welcome," she translated. A woman wearing a bright red *salwar-kameez* appeared in the doorway. "This is Uncle's wife," Hedwig said.

Uncle's wife gestured for us to sit down on the bed beneath the window. She and Uncle sat on the bed in the opposite corner. Their eyes flicked from my backpack to my muddy running shoes that had just left tracks across the freshly mopped floor.

"Is this their room?" I asked.

"Yes. But they are happy to move into another room."

Uncle and his wife smiled. I smiled back as best I could after a two-day journey by share jeep and bus along some of the most bone-shattering roads I'd ever encountered. Roads with potholes the size of a vehicle. Roads that had washed down cliff sides and were propped up by two-by-fours, entire families working alongside with pickaxes and hammers – making boulders into rocks and rocks into pebbles. Making new gravel as we'd waited to continue.

Suddenly, everyone got up and left me to settle in. "Uncle says to choose what you need from over there." Hedwig pointed to a pile of mattresses as thin as lawn chair cushions, a stack of a dozen pillows and matching comforters. "Dinner is at five. You will eat all of your meals at the school." Just as she turned to leave, the rain began. "I hope you brought an umbrella." She pointed to the door. "And a padlock."

I chose four mattresses and layered them one atop another. I toured the room, admiring the collection of flowered plastic teacups, saucers, and multi-sized serving dishes inside a wooden cabinet with sliding glass doors. One candle, one flashlight with batteries removed, two large copper vases. A lone high-heeled shoe in the corner. A piece of corncob.

The intensity of the rain increased until all other sound disappeared. The world became a perpetually gushing stream. I settled under the covers and tried to read.

It always felt strange, the arrival. It required an adjustment – time for the Me I was when the taxi dropped me off at the Kalimpong jeep stand days earlier to catch up with the Me I would become in this damp room in the foothills of Sikkim. I still felt dirty from the journey, especially from the night at Sonia's Guest House where the Juliet balcony had looked so promising. Too bad Sonia had been so drunk. Too bad the sheets were stained, and the toilet in the dark, dank bathroom wouldn't flush.

"Are you lonely?" Sonia had asked after knocking on my door. "Come," she'd beckoned. "Come." She'd wanted me to play cards and drink giant bottles of Cobra with the suspicious-looking men at the bar. Perhaps that's what the last occupant of the room had done, and look what had happened to the sheets. "You are family," she'd said. "Come."

I'd barricaded myself in the room. Luckily, thanks to my mother, I had a sleep sheet. But this had done nothing to protect me from the cockroaches, the noisy fan, the hole in the window screen that admitted thousands of mosquitoes when dusk hit, the all-night mantra-chanting at the Hindu temple next door.

It was important to carry a toolkit for the arrival – perhaps a Tibetan locket, a red journal, a slim volume of poetry by Billy Collins, a packet of incense. Something to set on top of a pretty piece of fabric on a cleared space of a dusty armoire to help you feel at home. I didn't know anything yet – if these people were kind, if the teenage boy staring at me through the window of my room was their son, if I should take a shower in the stall with a half door, if the children at the school would like me.

The rain stopped as suddenly as it began. Birds chirped. Cows lowed. Clouds slithered away above the treetops until the now even greener hillsides sparkled.

It was nearly time for dinner. I rummaged around in my backpack and found the padlock on the bottom. But what if Uncle's wife needed a teacup? What if they thought I didn't trust them?

I picked my way down the yellow-brick road slickened with rust-coloured mud and cow dung. Finally I arrived at the veranda of the blue cottage/schoolhouse and chose a plastic lawn chair beneath a mural of birds and flowers. Streamers rippled from the birds' wings, blowing in the breeze.

"Would you like *chai*?" the principal of Sikkim Himalayan Academy offered. He walked towards the cook shack where I could see Uncle stirring a pot as high as his waist.

A British accent floated through an open window of the classroom: "J is for jaywalking," the teacher said.

"Miss, what is jaywalking?" a student asked.

"Jaywalking is not obeying the traffic lights."

"Miss, what are traffic lights?"

The principal emerged from the kitchen shack. "Here you are," he said. "Forgive me, I must go. The dinner bell will ring soon."

I sipped the *chai*. I listened to the rushing river, bird song, the buzz of insects. Finally I'd reached the land of red panda and snow leopard, of ginger and black cardamom. A land the original inhabitants, the Lepcha, called Paradise. A vista of green stretched as far as the eye could see: bamboo, laurel, pine. The arrival was over. I was here.

"L is for ladies' fingers," the teacher said.

"Miss, what are ladies' fingers?"

"Okra. Uncle makes good okra, doesn't he?"

The students laughed.

I heard Hedwig's Dutch accent through the window to my left.

"Let's list the different types of suffering the young Buddha discovered when he left the palace," she said.

"Aging," said a student.

"Illness," said another.

"Death."

The dinner bell rang.

When I returned to my room later that night, I could tell someone had been visiting. *Sailing Alone Around the Room* was opened to a different page. My blankets were neatly folded. A stick of incense had burned down.

When I'd just about fallen asleep, I heard the pop of a bottle uncorking, a *glug, glug, glug*. Another *glug, glug, glug*. I heard the voices of Uncle and his wife as though they were right beside me. And they were. Light glowed through holes in the walls. Bugs flew back and forth freely. Uncle and his wife swigged. Coughed. Laughed. Sighed. *Glug, glug, glug*. I tried to remain as silent as possible on my mattresses.

The stopper uncorked as regularly as the monsoon poured down. Every night the voices grew louder and the sounds bolder. Every night Uncle and his wife yelled about things in the language of these grandiose mountains. Every morning I walked down the mountainside to the school and Uncle would bring me a cup of *chai*. Every morning I could smell the alcohol on his breath. From dawn to dusk he stirred the giant pots and scrubbed them by the spigot. We never looked one another in the eye. I wondered if I should tell Hedwig about Uncle's habit, but there was something about Uncle that kept me quiet.

There was something about this whole place that kept me quiet. Maybe it was one of the Indian teachers at the school who was paid twenty-five dollars a month, who'd grown up in one of Mother Teresa's houses in Darjeeling, whose parents were dead, who had a glass eye. Maybe it was the teenage boy with a basket strapped to his forehead who arrived at Uncle's every morning at 5:30 a.m., singing at the top of his lungs.

"Does Uncle have children?" I'd asked Hedwig.

"Not anymore," she'd ansuewered.

Maybe it was the children at the school, who brought me plates filled with *dal* and rice, saying, "Enjoy your meal, Angela Miss."

Maybe it was the little girls who always wanted to braid my hair: "It is like gold, Angela Miss"; the little boys who stood so quietly with bowed heads as the principal checked for lice, or shaved their heads to heal their painful-looking sores.

The day of departure arrived. I left an envelope on the dresser of my room with three times the agreed rate. When I walked down the yellow brick road to catch the first bus of the day, Uncle was waiting with a cup of *chai* and a packet of biscuits. The bus arrived. Honked. Uncle swung my backpack onto his shoulders. We looked at one another then, neither of us knowing the right words.

Soon the bus turned the first bend and cliffs merged seamlessly into valleys. Here, Hedwig had told me, you could see clear across to Darjeeling. In the morning light, the landscape shimmered with silvery threads of streams and golden spires of monasteries. I opened the biscuits.

THE TRAVEL HUSBAND

THE ALARM WENT OFF AT 3:30 A.M. Immediately, I opened the curtains to look outside. Thick clouds hid Darjeeling from view. Slowly they edged across Chowrasta Main Square, revealing the dark shape of a fountain, a sleeping dog. We wouldn't be able to see a thing, I thought. But still I got dressed. I packed a few bananas and a bottle of water. I tested my flashlight, then opened the heavy wooden door leading into the hallway. Kurt was already there, waiting on the jute mat. We didn't speak.

We descended into the dark, damp morning casting beams of light across façades of hotels and shuttered shop fronts. Rope-lashed tarps protected vendors' stalls from the perils of the night. Piles of refuse awaited garbage pickers. In the distance, a pack of dogs began a frenzied chorus of barking.

"Tiger Hill?" A man approached from the shadows.

"Yes," Kurt said, asking how much. It was one of Kurt's jobs, as travel husband, to negotiate prices.

Other lone women travellers had touted the benefits of a travel husband – a male tourist who understood that India was, for the most part, still a world run by men, and who wanted to help. Kurt, a software designer from Belgium, was my second travel husband. Cyrille from Paris, whom I'd met in Ladakh's Nubra Valley, had been my first. With something as simple as a travel husband by her side, a woman could relax a little. The millions of staring men so fond of engaging in conversation on the streets of India became more bearable. A woman could travel to the remote regions of northern India and hike across the sand dunes to Diskit, or explore the rhododendron forests of South Sikkim, and feel a little more at ease. It was a relationship of mutual benefit – cheaper room rates and transportation costs, and a little bit of company with no strings attached.

"Wait here," the man said. "We leave soon."

He escorted us to the back seat of his jeep, into the ice-blue glow cast by the interior lights. Dance music pumped out of his souped-up stereo at a volume much too high for this hour. "Do you think he'd mind if we turned it down?" I asked Kurt. Kurt turned it off.

The driver blended into the darkness with his black leather coat and jeans. I watched as the glow of his cell phone moved towards the door of the Olde Bellevue Hotel. I knew what he was doing – fishing for sleepy tourists. "Tiger Hill?" he asked over and over. But they were more organized than us. They'd already booked their "organized sunrise trip" at Clubside taxi stand yesterday.

"He's not going to leave until the jeep is full," I said. Full, I'd learned, meant at least double a jeep's recommended seating capacity. It wasn't called a "share jeep" for no reason. You shared everything. Body parts, sneezes, sweat.

"Let's wait and see," said Kurt.

Fifteen minutes passed and we were still alone. This was my last day in Darjeeling, my last chance to see Tiger Hill. Finally the monsoon had been over long enough to be guaranteed a view of a 250-kilometre stretch of Himalayan peaks – including Everest – light up in the sunrise. A sight even the most jaded of travellers had recommended.

"Let's offer to pay for all the seats so we can just go," I suggested. But Kurt wouldn't hear of it. "It won't cost that much," I said.

I'd learned the Indian rupee became more than just a type of currency to some tourists. The well-worn bills became their pride. They began to forget, after a relatively short time in India, that they were haggling for mere pennies. I'd witnessed several embarrassing interactions between westerners and Tibetan refugees who were selling hand-knit woolen socks for the equivalent of a dollar, for example. "Twenty-five rupees," the westerner insisted. I'm certain they'd read the same thing I'd read in my guidebook, to begin bargaining by offering half the asked-for price. But they'd forgotten the part about how this woman had walked hundreds of miles through the Himalayas to arrive at the refugee camp on the other side of the hill. Hence the wind-burned cheeks, the cracked skin on her palms. "Twenty-five," the westerner had insisted and the woman took the money, too desperate to refuse.

Bargaining became a matter of principle for some. People seemed to loathe the thought that someone could be screwing them. They yelled, swore, much to the amusement of the locals.

"No," Kurt said. "Let's wait."

"I'll pay." But I knew this suggestion was futile. The leather coat man would begin to wonder about Kurt's masculinity. He'd look at the bills handed to him by a woman in the ice-blue glow, and then look at Kurt and smile.

Another fifteen minutes passed. I imagined I saw the sky lighten, though the cloud-cover was so thick it was hard to tell. "I'm leaving," I said. I didn't care about wandering the dark streets alone anymore. When would I ever have the chance to see some of the highest peaks in the world light up one by one again? Kurt looked at the leather jacket man and yelled, "We're leaving!" The man waved his glowing cell phone in reply.

We hurried down the cobblestone path to Clubside, where we hoped a few stray share jeeps would be lying in wait. A woman wearing a heavy cardigan poured *chai* from a thermos into plastic shooter cups, serving a handful of drivers. "Tiger Hill?" they asked half-heartedly. One of them gestured towards his jeep.

"When are you leaving?" Kurt tapped his watch.

"Two minutes."

"How much?"

The driver didn't answer. He could smell our desperation. He knew he had us.

The jeep was almost full. Burly Australians who still stank of booze from the night before. They sat in the back, boasting of their bargaining conquests on the subcontinent. "He said 1,000 and I said 500. No way I'd pay more than 500."

Five minutes ticked by. Ten. Now I knew I wasn't imagining things: the sky really was lightening. The only tourists who would arrive at this hour would be the ones even more stubborn than us. The anti-tourist-site tourists. The ones who spent their days drinking tea and reading the *Times of India* like modern-day versions of the British Raj. The ones who scorned all those who came to India to see things like the Taj Mahal.

Finally, two lone women sauntered down the hill toward the jeep. "Tiger Hill?" the driver asked. The Australians were delighted as the women squished into the back seat.

"Can we go now?" I hissed to Kurt. He got out of the jeep and tapped the driver on the shoulder. But you should never rush a man who is drinking his morning *chai* in India. The driver ignored him and made us wait another five minutes. Of course we were never going to see Tiger

Hill now.

The stories of bargaining escalated in volume now that the two women had arrived. I was just about to open the door and go back to the hotel when the driver appeared, suddenly bursting with energy. He looked at his watch and lurched out of the parking lot. He attached his hand to the horn, squealing around corners, scattering vendors trying to make their way to the market. He was heedless of the oncoming traffic, mostly cargo trucks at this hour, also in a hurry, careening down the pot-holed, monsoon-ravaged, barely paved road. The Australians began to tell tales of the crazy drivers of India.

We were the last jeep to arrive, passing hundreds of other jeeps parked on the side of the road. Luckily our driver had connections and continued right up to the compound where only special tour jeeps were allowed. He slid into a spot.

Everyone had already taken their places. The viewing pavilion was built like a triple layer cake made of cinder block and glass. It was easy to tell the people on the top layer in the heated lounge had been there awhile, clearly enjoying their cups of complimentary *chai*. The two bottom layers were warmed by body heat. Children were passed from one set of shoulders to another, and the Indian tourists, clearly accustomed to being awake at such an hour, became excited by the smallest break in the clouds. "Where are you from?" they asked. "Are you married? Any children?"

The general-viewing inner sanctum quickly became claustrophobic. We went outside where more hordes had gathered, climbing fire escapes, pressing against railings. Cameras stood poised, clicking madly at anything that moved. A woman called up from the parking lot, "*Chai! Chai!*"

I held the warm shooter cup and drank it in one gulp. "Another?" she asked.

A young girl from Bangalore encouraged me to climb with her to the top rungs of the fire escape while the security guard looked the other way. We hung from the ladder, feeling the chill of the high-elevation clouds – snow clouds, she told me they were called – passing through us. A dime-sized orange sphere began to burn through the clouds. Chatter subsided. Camera shutters opened. Click, click, click.

Suddenly a cheer rose up, the kind of cheer I'd only heard in India –
joyous, heart-felt, loud. The girl and I looked and looked at the orange
disc and wondered what all the fuss was about. Then we heard a collective
intake of breath and a chorus of Oooohs and Ahhhhhs.

"Pema!!" the girl's mother yelled. "Other side! Other side!"

Quickly we climbed down the ladder and pushed our way through to
the other side. And there they were, shedding clouds like the blankets
of waking giants, rising above the valley like another universe. But it
wasn't over yet. Khangchendzonga, the great five-peaked snow fortress,
the third- highest peak in the world, began to glow in a rose-coloured
light. One by one, other peaks began to glow. Just as the *Lonely Planet*
had promised.

As the sun rose higher, the peaks grew brighter, filling the horizon
with a blinding white light. Darjeeling lay below, a city made of toy
blocks. I had one of those moments when your heart skips a beat. I'd felt
it before – standing on the edge of the Grand Canyon, walking beneath
the pillars of the Acropolis. But this was different. Now I knew why I
did this – why I packed up everything in boxes over and over and said
my good-byes. It was to stand here with strangers, all facing the same
direction, knowing for certain this time that we were just specks in the
universe. But that we were specks together.

THE YOUNG WOMAN

I DIDN'T SEE HER AT FIRST. I was too caught up in the chanting of *Om Mani Padme Om*. "Are you married?" she asked. She wore a sari the colour of lapis lazuli. Her hair shone with coconut oil and good health. She was young, barely twenty.

I decided to tell her the truth. "No," I said, touching my fake wedding ring.

A group of Tibetan refugees walked past chanting *Om Mani Padme Om*.

"Even though I'm not Buddhist, I come here when I feel like I can't go on," she said waving towards the *bodhi* tree. Her hand shook a little. "I dream to be like you. Free to be independent. To see the world. To do anything I want."

A group of beggars arrived behind the wrought-iron gate surrounding Bodh Gaya's Mahabodhi Temple. They poked bony wrists through the openings and flipped open their palms. "Rupee, please?" they asked. "Madame! Madame!" they called. Some held tin bowls, clanging them against the bars.

More Tibetans circled. *Om Mani Padme Om*. Nearly every one of them dropped something into the palms and tin bowls, even those who looked like they'd just crossed the Himalayas by foot. I listened to the *clink, clink, clink* of coins hitting tin.

I noticed the young woman's eyes welling up with tears. She lowered her head. "Forgive me for bothering you. It means so much to me that you were willing to talk," she said, placing her palms between her chest. "*Namaste*."

She was gone before I could give her my hotel's address, invite her for dinner, tell her she wasn't alone.

I circled until the colours of the sky began to shift hues, until the birds settled into the branches for one last burst of song. *Om Mani Padme Om*.

I walked back outside the temple gate, back into India. Suddenly, I was overwhelmed by this world: the stray dogs, the cows, the heat, the man pushing himself along the pavement on stumps, the reception line of women and children in filthy clothing sitting listlessly on the pavement where they lived, the calls of the vendors, the blaring Hindi music, the rickshaw motors, the bus growls, the diesel fumes.

I sat down to drink a *chai*. Soon the beggars swarmed around me, but the *chai*-stand owner uttered one harsh-sounding syllable, and they dispersed.

THE BEGGARS

1. Barefoot Girl

DON'T GIVE TO THE BEGGARS, they tell me, especially the children, especially the little girl who stares as I take a bite of chocolate-mocha torte, her eyes like riverbed stones. The little barefoot girl in a once-powder-blue party dress, with once-white-lace ruffles. A dress made to fit snug on the shoulders, to graze the bottom of the knee, to zip up the back and be accompanied by white tights and patent leather shoes. A dress made for a girl twice her age, for a girl who has tasted birthday cake. Don't give to the beggars, they tell me. I chew. Swipe away a crumb.

2. Eyes Too Bright

WALK. WALK BRISKLY. Hold head high.. Ignore the man with stumps for legs propelling himself along with stumps for hands on a board with wheels, pushing through the cow dung, betel nut spit, puddles of dirty water. Ignore that he's the same height as the rib cages of those feral dogs fighting over mouldy *chapatis*. Ignore that his stumps are so worn they shine. Don't make eye contact. His eyes are too bright. Too beautiful. Walk even more briskly. He's catching up. Run. Run if you have to. Run.

3. Milk, Please

I ORDER CHAI BY THE TEMPLE. They appear from behind the stands that sell prayer flags – a young boy holding a baby girl in his arms. They watch me, and I am used to this by now. I hold the glass, listening to mantras play on the loudspeakers, watching the flags droop in the heat. Four eyes follow the route of glass rim to the edge of lips. I sip, and the boy's mantra begins: Rupee please, biscuits please. Milk. Please. I sip. The baby's lips are so dry. I sip. Her cheeks so caked with the filth of all of this.

THE DOCTOR

First we stopped for samosas, then *chai*. Then we picked up the pharmacist.

"Our medicine man," the doctor joked. The nurse giggled. The jeep drove past the mud huts and thatched roofs of the Bihar Plains, heading to where we would set up the weekly mobile clinic in the countryside surrounding Bodh Gaya.

The villagers waited on the veranda of a building fronted by Roman columns, its once periwinkle walls stained by the soot of the highway. They waited, jiggling babies on hips, leaning on canes, sitting against the walls staring at the highway. The pharmacist swept out the building with a broom made of twigs. The doctor set his briefcase on a rusty metal desk and arranged his files. The nurse wandered among the villagers, handing out colour-coded cards: pink for urgent, yellow for less-urgent. And then she distributed the numbers. Who arrived first this morning? A woman in a turquoise sari holding the hand of a very pale boy raised her pink card in the air. She had arrived at dawn.

The villagers had the patience of the water buffalo that grazed these surrounding fields, enduring the heat, the mosquitoes, and the dust with an unnerving calm. Perhaps they had the patience of those who didn't have much to wait for. Skin stretched taut over bone. Clothing hung loose. But smiles came easily; the doctors had come to their village.

The pharmacist spread a large piece of burlap on the dirt floor, opened a large wooden case, and propped it up like a medicine cabinet to face him. He arranged brown glass bottles with hand-printed labels: *Artemisia absinthium, Piper longum, Carthamus tinctorius.* He filled plastic vials with tiny white sugar pills. From a cardboard box, he unpacked containers of mineral salts: magnesium, potassium, calcium, iron. He settled himself cross-legged on the burlap, looked at the doctor, then the nurse, and nodded. The woman in turquoise entered and stood before the doctor, speaking with a soft voice, her eyes downcast. The little boy wrapped himself around her leg, buried his face into the folds of her sari. The doctor wrote a prescription on a white slip. The woman passed the slip to the pharmacist, her eyes still downcast, the boy still hiding from view, and the day began.

The second patient arrived – an old man leaning on a wooden cane. Every step looked painful. The doctor worked quickly. He ripped a white slip from his notepad. The old man passed it to the pharmacist with a shaky hand. Seven droplets of *Annona reticulata* absorbed into the sugar pills. He explained to the man what he must do. The man looked confused, and the pharmacist explained again. The man looked at him helplessly. But the next slip had arrived. "Go now my friend, go now," the pharmacist said. The old man limped toward the wall, slumping down to rest on his haunches, turning the plastic vial round and round in his hands. Next, a young woman in a marigold-orange sari waited as the pharmacist shook a packet of mineral salts. She held her palms between her chest in prayer position, her head bowed. The pharmacist explained, "You must drink this mixture in water three times per day."

The woman nodded her head. "Thank you sir, thank you sir." She backed away, palms still together.

Soon the white slips began to pile up. The pharmacist shook and measured. The patients watched and bowed. Fever. Malnutrition. Infertility. The pharmacist sealed the vials. Explained what to do as more and more patients arrived. Depression. Rheumatism. Anemia. Outside, transport trucks and buses honked every few seconds, sending plumes of diesel fumes onto the veranda. The vehicles drove quickly through Bandha, quickly through the entire state of Bihar, a state known for its bandits, militants, and corrupt officials. But the young girl awaiting her prescription was oblivious to the highway. She soothed the baby in her arms, patting the sweat from its brow with the edge of a threadbare shawl. With kohl-rimmed eyes, she stared curiously at the bottle of *Ocimum sanctum* in the pharmacist's hands.

Finally the doctor stopped, looked at the others. It was time for lunch. They walked outside to a spigot and took turns washing hands while the other pumped. The nurse closed the clinic doors. The room cooled instantly. Another piece of burlap was laid upon the ground. A tower of stainless steel tins was dismantled and the containers passed around to be shared. *Dal.* Basmati rice. *Aloo gobi.* The doctor sliced a cucumber. The nurse, a tomato. The pharmacist, a lemon. They distributed small green chilies. Lunch began. The doctor talked about the old man. Fifty-years old. Tuberculosis. Soon he would die. The little boy? Leukemia, undiagnosed for too long. They didn't have any equipment beyond a stethoscope. He too would die soon. The doctor bit the tip of a chili. There was nothing they could do but offer sugar pills, and tiny droplets of hope.

Within half an hour lunch was over and the burlap folded. The pharmacist settled himself cross-legged in front of his cabinet; the doctor arranged his files. They nodded at the nurse. She opened the doors and the bright light of Bandha flooded the room. A girl with stunning long-lashed eyes had been waiting to collect the leftovers. She walked awkwardly across the veranda, legs twisted from polio. The villagers divided the *chapatis* into halves. They had their own system of distributing the food, their own order of urgency. The children received the largest portions. The old man was next. Most ate nothing. The nurse called the next number, and the afternoon began.

THE VILLAGERS

LUCKILY, JESSICA SPOKE HINDI. "Come to the village," the girl with legs twisted from polio said. From our piece of burlap spread on the cement floor, we looked towards the doctor. He shrugged.

"Enjoy," he said, rifling through a sheaf of dog-eared files. "Volunteers have been there before. It's safe."

Jessica and I stopped filling vials with glucose pills. We pulled aside the curtain of the mobile clinic and stood on the veranda with the waiting patients. The girl positioned herself between us. She took our hands. As we entered the sunshine, a group of barefoot children fell into line behind us. We crossed a dusty field filled with a few scrawny water buffalo and tufts of grass, traversing the highway and a ditch filled with garbage. We arrived to not much more than a smattering of mud-and-wattle huts the same ochre colour as the surrounding countryside, walls patterned with pats of buffalo dung left to dry in the sun.

The children whispered. I didn't need to understand the language to know they were talking about us. They fanned out into a semi-circle. They spotted my watch, Jessica's blue eyes. But they were too polite to stare too long at one place. They took us in as though we were paintings, eyes darting from one blotch of colour to another.

"This way," the girl, clearly their leader, commanded when she felt they'd looked enough. She led us to a dried-up river gulch where a Hindu temple rose from its banks. A weather-worn façade writhed with the body parts of goddesses. Banyan roots twisted into its foundations, cracking open the sandstone. I smelled incense. Damp earth. Something too ancient to name.

"Let's go back," I whispered to Jessica, but our leader had already entered. The other children stood at the threshold, encouraging us to step across.

Some travellers instinct kicked in. A wariness of dark unknown places where anyone could be hiding. I reminded myself this was India, and India's poorest state. But the children smiled. Go, go, they gestured, puzzled by such hesitation.

"Let's go," Jessica said, and entered the gloom. The children stayed behind.

When my eyes adjusted to the darkness, I saw the bats. They hung from the upper reaches of domes, or swooped from one stone goddess to another. It was difficult not to step in their guano. Next, I saw a long white beard and bare torso.

"Sadhu," our leader whispered. Holy man.

Somewhere from within the folds of her dress, she produced an offering. She laid a coin in a stone receptacle filled with marigold blossoms. The sadhu didn't look up from the flames of his small fire. Our leader stared at us. We rummaged around in our money belts. Her eyes took in the crisp bills we placed beside her coin. "Go," she said, gesturing towards the entrance. A few moments later, she followed.

The children awaited us in the sunshine. Their numbers had swelled. We walked back in the direction of the huts where women stood in dark doorways. Two plastic chairs had been set up in a small clearing.

"Sit, sit!" our leader commanded. We sat. The children giggled. Our leader addressed Jessica.

"They want to know if you're a movie star," Jessica translated. I smiled and shook my head. The children looked a little disappointed. "Maybe it's the sunglasses," Jessica said, and I realized I'd forgotten to take them off. A woman stepped forward from a dark doorway. "She wants to know if you're married." When I started to shake my head, Jessica advised: "Say yes." I nodded. Everyone looked relieved. Other women stepped forward from other dark doorways. The questions continued: "How old are you?" "Where are your children?" "Where is your husband?" "Father?" "Brother?" "Why have they left you alone?"

Suddenly our leader announced it was time to move on. Two children were delegated the task of carrying our chairs. More and more villagers joined in the procession. We rounded a bend where a low wall sat in front of a roofless building made of cinder blocks.

"That's the school," Jessica translated as we settled into our chairs. "Now they're asking if you like sugar-cane."

"I love it," I said, and nodded enthusiastically. Everyone smiled at this new tidbit of information. I waited. Would they serve it with freshly squeezed lime?

But no one moved. The villagers stared. "What's going on?" I whispered to Jessica. The leader spoke.

"Oh," Jessica turned and looked at me. She laughed. "I made a mistake. They said *singing*, not sugar cane. They're waiting for a song."

"But I can't sing."

"You have to. Just sing anything. I'll sing along if I know it."

I looked out at the villagers' expectant faces, took a deep breath, and sang the first thing that came to mind. Jessica shot me a puzzled look. "Jingle bells! Jingle bells!" we sang.

The villagers clapped. "Again!" they demanded. "Again!" And so we sang. At first it was a little boy who figured out the words and sang along to the chorus. Then it was the whole village. They sang, heedless of pronunciation. They sang, gustily, with perfect pitch. Frosty the Snowman. Rudolph. Jessica and I sang louder. We rose from our chairs and held out our arms to the hot afternoon sun.

"Thank you," our leader said after the first verse of "Deck the Halls." The villagers nodded their heads in agreement. Some clasped hands in front of their chests and bowed. The chairs were whisked away. The women returned to their doorways. It was time to go.

The leader took her place between Jessica and me. She limped along slowly, the full weight of every moment sinking in. We'd move on, far away from this village, and these children would remain here. I looked at their bare feet and tattered clothing. I felt the warmth of one of their hands in mine. They led us safely through the barren fields, past the barking dogs, across the pot-holed highway. When we arrived back at the makeshift clinic, the children dispersed. No one said good-bye.

THE MEDITATION TEACHER

"PLEASE LEAVE SHOES HERE," read the sign beside the door of the *gompa* at the Root Institute for Wisdom Culture. I placed my flip-flops neatly beside the others, slid the wooden door closed, and entered another world. Gone was the birdsong, the rumble of bus and rickshaw, the Hindi pop music, the laughter of children running through the rice fields. Even the air changed. Dry. Cool. The smell of cedar, cinnamon, of wet spring leaves. I looked at the others already sitting on their meditation cushions, cross-legged, eyes closed.

A woman with short black hair sat at the front of the room on a slightly raised dais. She wore a long burgundy robe cinched at the waist. To her right sat a small brass bowl, a bouquet of dahlias, a glass of water, a tape recorder. She smiled and gestured towards the cushions placed strategically throughout the room. Which place should I choose?

Everyone looked so vulnerable with closed eyes – the young man with full lips and long dark lashes, the older man with the salt-and-pepper beard and purple cotton pants, the red-haired woman brushing a strand of hair from her forehead. A woman in the back still had her eyes open. I noted her greying bob and the Kashmiri shawl draped around her shoulders. She stared out the window at the *pipal* tree. I walked towards the empty cushion beside her.

Each time the door slid open a new retreatant entered. One of the four women I was sharing a dorm with came in – *Deva*, originally from Mumbai, now living in Cologne. I admired her shimmery black hair and ruby nose ring. She settled on a cushion in front of the altar, framed by flowers and golden light cast from the statue of the Buddha.

I closed my eyes, listening to the door slide open and closed, to the other retreatants settling into their cushions, to the gardeners speaking Hindi to one another outside.

It was time for the introductions. The woman on the dais was from Amsterdam. "Think of me as a nun without the shaved head," she laughed.

Yosef from Israel. Jessica from America. Neil from Australia.

"I'm crazy for the *dharma*."

"My boyfriend broke his leg and now we're stuck here for awhile."

"I don't know anything about Buddhism and have no idea why I'm here."

It was my turn next. I hated these kind of things and could already feel the colour rising to my cheeks. "I'm here because of a leaf," I said and instantly regretted it. Everyone turned to look at me. "A *bodhi* leaf, at the temple."

~

THERE WAS NO WIND. The air was still and hot. I sat on a bench beneath an ancient *bodhi* tree and concentrated on the foliage above my head, willing a leaf to fall. If a leaf fell, I'd promised myself to learn about the man who'd sat here over 2,500 years ago and supposedly attained nirvana.

To be honest, I didn't know why I'd made such a promise. I'd never really been interested in Buddhism – or any other religion – before now. And I had serious doubts about eternal bliss. But this was India. I'd learned this was the type of thing you did here, and to forget about what I used to think.

My concept of normality had shifted the moment my cab pulled out of Indira Gandhi International Airport: cows lounged in the middle of the roundabout blocking traffic; a beggar-woman held what looked like a dead baby in her arms. When the taxi stopped at a red light, she'd jutted her bundle through the open window: "Milk, please. Milk, please. Madame. Please."

My eyes were closed. I opened them sporadically, curious about the commotion around me. A group of people dressed in grey robes circled Mahabodhi Temple in a clockwise direction, chanting. An old woman in a long red dress and colourfully striped apron fell to her knees, slid herself prostrate, and touched her forehead to the white marble walkway. She stood, brushed the dirt from her apron, adjusted her braids, and began again. Hindu tourists jingled bangles and anklets, posing for photos in their jewel-toned saris as close as they could get to the glassed-in *bodhi* tree trunk. A skinny guard with a long wooden baton shooed away little beggar boys who alit like fruit flies upon offerings of cookies and cakes. Birds chirped. A loudspeaker played the same monotone chant over and over again. I sat. Waited.

The next time I opened my eyes, a group of monks in brick-coloured robes sat cross-legged on the marble, eyes closed in meditation. Other monks began to settle around me as gracefully as a flock of birds. Everyone else, even the beggars, had disappeared. I decided it was time to give up this silly game.

As I wove through the spaces left between monks, I saw it, fluttering down from the *bodhi* tree's upper branches.

I watched it fall like the first snowflake of winter. It landed on the toe of my right foot. I looked around, smiling, wondering if anyone else had witnessed this little miracle.

"That one's meant for you." I turned to see a monk smiling so mischievously I almost thought he was flirting. But then he laughed, the innocent laugh of a child.

"Do you really think so?" I bent to pick up the heart-shaped leaf with tiny, interconnecting veins.

The monk stopped laughing. "I know so," he said and walked away.

I moved to the outermost pathway of the temple, where the circular flow continued. There were more old women with braids, more prostrating, more beggars, more tourists. There was a painter's palette of robes: maroon, white, saffron, grey, orange. There were *bodhi* trees and palm trees, and islands of statues adorned with marigold blossoms. The chanting on the loudspeakers rose above it all. I ran a finger up and down the stem of the leaf and joined the flow.

~

"EVERYBODY READY TO SUFFER?" the woman on the dais asked. We all laughed nervously. "Most of us think sitting still for forty-five minutes on a cushion will be a pleasant experience." She straightened her back, adjusted her robes. The pixie-like, sparkly-eyed big sister disappeared. "Let's get into meditation position. Cross your legs. Think as though you are building the foundation of a house." She waited a moment. "Relax your spine. Your mouth. Your brow. Keep your eyes closed."

A gong sounded. It moved like a wave throughout the room, vibrating until it disappeared.

"Watch your thoughts pass like clouds in the sky. One after the other."

We woke every morning in the darkness at 6 a.m. and went to sit on our cushions. We'd been discouraged from speaking; we'd been assured it was all part of going inwards. In silence, we ate in the garden alongside a trio of goats the retreat centre had saved from being slaughtered as a Hindu sacrifice. In silence, we walked from the mediation hall to our rooms and back again along white stone pathways.

In silence, my body ached and my mind became a separate entity I no longer wished to associate with. It developed crushes on unlikely members of our group: the much older Hans from Germany, the much younger Yosef from Israel. I became jealous of anyone better looking (*Deva*), or who'd had the sense to bring comfy yoga pants (everyone). Annoyance festered at the way people ate, walked, washed their dishes, coughed. The only beings that didn't annoy me were the goats. Every day I fed them my papaya peels after breakfast, whispering endearments lest I got caught speaking.

Every evening, I walked in the darkness to the communal bathroom to brush my teeth. Then I climbed under my mosquito net and tucked the edges snug under the mattress. The person closest to the light switch was in charge of waiting until exactly 9:30 p.m. until she plunged us into darkness. Each of us alone in our fine-meshed cocoons. Our beds so close we could hear the rise and fall of one another's breath. But we were strangers now beneath the cloak of silence. Invisible. We kept our heads down, mindful of the loudness of a footstep, a door closing, a suitcase unzipping, a page turning.

At the end of Day Three, the cicadas began their noisy chorus. Then a feeling I thought I'd left on the other side of the world found me again. Dark and heavy as the humid night. Now I understood why they'd asked about the state of our mental health on the registration form. I understood why a woman in the last retreat had jumped from the rooftop of her third-floor dormitory. Going inwards could be deadly.

The feeling was as stealthy as the mosquito that found her way into my cocoon every night. Once the feeling had stayed with me for weeks. I hadn't wanted to open the curtains in the morning. Or eat. Or be alive. And here in Bodh Gaya, I heard Michel's voice again, echoing from eight years earlier. "You're weak!" he yelled. "You're so insecure!" He slammed his fist on the kitchen table. "Don't you get it?" he said, grabbing my

121

shoulders and shaking me. "You're empty inside!"

I felt myself shrinking smaller and smaller. The mosquito net billowed around me like a new universe. I was terrified. Terrified of the void. For years I'd done anything to avoid it. Drank too much. Surrounded myself with overly positive people. Had sex with inappropriate men. Holed up on remote islands. Flown to Paris. Flown to Cancún. Flown to Delhi. I'd charged it to my credit card. I'd waitressed until my feet ached.

I tried not to cry. I knew they'd hear me. They were shifting too much to be sleeping. They'd know the truth if I cried. They'd know Michel had been right. I was weak. Insecure. Empty. That should be my mantra.

A mosquito buzzed. I broke Rule Number One: *No Killing*, and killed it with an angry slap. I felt like hitting everything – my pillow, *Deva*, the concrete walls. I wanted to run screaming from the room and into the night. I hugged my pillow to my chest, squeezing it so hard my arms hurt. I tried to do what the woman on the dais had taught us: breathe. *Inhale-One-Exhale-One.* Michel yelling, "You're crazy. You're just like my mother!" *Inhale-Two-Exhale-Two.* Michel and the one-night stands, the tree planting cook, the eighteen-year-old rideshare passenger, the German tourist, the pottery school classmate. *Inhale-Three- Exhale-Three.* "Why do you imagine things? What's wrong with you?" *Inhale-Four-Exhale-Four.* The yelling. Every day. Our neighbour in the courtyard, me on the fire escape. "*Ça va?*" she asks, looking up. Are you okay?

I thought of the *bodhi* leaf pressed between the pages of my guidebook. The only reason I was still here was because of that stupid leaf. I thought it had been a sign. But everyone here had one. Some overlaid with gold leaf, others laminated. You could buy them from the gift shop at Mahabodhi Temple, or from young monks who pulled them out from the folds of their robes, whispering a price.

I'd been a fool to believe in signs. To believe India could be different than the other places. That I could wear a necklace of *rudraksha* seeds and be married within the year. That I could eat yak butter and never get sick again. That I could wash away bad karma in a river. That Friday was my lucky day and six my lucky number. That a bracelet blessed by the Dalai Lama could protect me from the evil of an invisible force. That I should wear a diamond and the colour cream. The only thing I'd learned in India was that life really was just suffering. The woman on the dais reminded us of this several times a day.

"The Buddha's first Noble Truth," she said. "Life is suffering."

Before we retired for the evening, she never failed to remind us of the biggest suffering of all: Death. "See you in the morning," she said. "If you're still here."

But then, on Day Seven, something changed.

"Good morning, everyone," the woman on the dais said. "I'm really happy to see you again." We got into meditation position. She rang the gong. I listened to the birds chirping, so loud this time of the morning. Thoughts passed like clouds. My mother crying at the departure gate when I flew from Toronto to Delhi. The man beside me coughing – why did he always start coughing as soon as the gong sounded?

"The Buddha said there are four basic things we need in life: food, clothing, shelter, medicine," said the woman on the dais. "If you have those four things, one should simply try to be content. To have a contented mind, a calm mind." I shifted on my cushion. She continued, "Our mind is like an endless movie filled with thoughts. Don't engage with them. The problem is not so much that there are thoughts, the problem is that we believe them." The woman on the dais cleared her throat. I stretched my neck – to the left, to the right. "The past does not exist," she said. "It's merely a thought in the present. The only reality is the present moment."

I stopped shifting and stretching and listened. I'd heard it all before, but now it began to sink into me like a stone in water.

During breakfast, I began to notice things I hadn't noticed before. The elderly gardener in a turban cradling a giant dahlia blossom in his hands. The velvety texture of papaya on my tongue. The bald man carrying a tray of freshly-cut fruit. How gently he placed the tray on the table, as though it were laden with delicate crystal. At 9:30 p.m., I enclosed myself in the mosquito netting and slept like I'd never slept before.

At the 6:45 a.m. meditation session, I was able to sit for the full forty-five minutes without shards of pain piercing my neck and my feet turning to stone. The woman on the dais fixed me with a stare of her clear blue eyes and smiled.

The feeling of lightness continued through to Day Eight. Day Nine.

I actually began to enjoy waking at six o'clock in the morning. On Day Ten we took photos, exchanged email addresses. Anna left for Varanasi, Yosef headed to Kathmandu, *Deva* to Goa. But my backpack remained stowed beneath the bed. I couldn't decide where to go next. I flipped through my guidebook, reading of cave murals and tiger reserves. I flipped to the *bodhi* leaf. Traced the edge of the heart. I held it to the light, examining the tiny, interconnecting veins.

I thought of the woman on the dais, riding off on her bicycle to visit Mahabodhi Temple, her eyes as bright as the strings of prayer flags strung across the front gate.

I thought of the bald man. That afternoon, he'd asked why I'd come here. "Because a *bodhi* leaf fell at my feet." I'd laughed.

"It was a sign," he'd said. The temple bells began to ring. "Where are you going next?"

I looked towards the rice fields, to the dusty hills in the distance. Along the footpaths, young monks in brick-red robes played tag. "Nowhere," I said.

THE VOLUNTEER

IT WAS THE ACCENT THAT GOT ME at first. I was a sucker for an accent: French, Spanish, Irish. I'd had relationships with men of all those nationalities and never tired of the way they rolled their R's or elongated their vowels. "Say it again," I'd begged. This was serious business – the headiest of aphrodisiacs. And this guy, the guy with a bald head who was just about to sell me a chocolate bar, was none other than Italian.

"Chocolate is my only weakness," I said stupidly, nervous in the face of the most beautiful accent in the world.

"Then let me buy it for you," he said, and I felt as though I'd just sucked back a dozen raw oysters. I stared into his lovely Mediterranean eyes. There was no going back.

It didn't matter that we were at a Buddhist retreat centre where a large sign dominating the front gate listed seven rules: "Number Four: Be Celibate: No sexual activity." It didn't matter that he was a long-term volunteer with an eye on monkhood.

The retreat was over. He was Italian. His name was Giuseppe. He indulged my chocolate weakness. He took me out for lunch at the Tibetan place that sold *momos*. He told me he was a jazz musician. He made love to me in a three-dollar-a-night hotel beside a swamp where mosquitoes bred and families of pigs wallowed. He called me *bellissima*.

He asked if I'd wait for him while he completed a month-long silent retreat at the centre, which was due to commence in two days' time. I hesitated. "I won't go if you say no," he said.

No, I felt like saying, but stopped myself. "If it's important to you, you should go," I said, trying to sound casual, trying on a new way of being that recommended rejoicing in the happiness of others no matter how much you wanted them to pack up their meditation cushion and visit the Taj Mahal with you. Buddhists called this love. I called it difficult. The Italian looked at me, pleased. I felt as though I'd passed some kind of test.

"Then we shouldn't waste any time," he said, brushing away the mosquitoes congregating above our pillows.

I waited. I checked out of my retreat dormitory and into a one-room adobe hut beside a patch of grass where the gardener tethered the goats after breakfast. From here I could watch the retreatants gather to enter the main *gompa* – a flat-roofed temple filled with colourful Tibetan Buddhist hangings, golden statues, and red cushions. The gong sounded. It was time for round two of meditation and chanting. I tried to catch a glimpse of my lover's bald head as he slipped out of his flip-flops and entered the main doors.

The retreatants were under strict orders for the month. Not only were they forbidden to speak, they were forbidden to make any kind of gesture. No eye contact. No smiles. They'd been encouraged to keep their gaze either averted or lowered, and focus on the present moment. They'd been encouraged to examine the leaves in the *bodhi* trees flickering in the wind, the birds chirping in their boughs, while keeping in mind the impermanent, suffering, and non-self nature of such phenomena. But under no circumstances were they to examine their new girlfriend peeking out from behind the curtains of her hut.

Signs were posted all over the grounds warning visitors: "Retreat in Progress. Strict silence enforced." The centre's spiritual director from Minnesota constantly made the rounds in her traditional Tibetan white blouse and brick-coloured, ankle-length skirt, glaring at those who showed signs of wanting to communicate.

After a few days, my resolve to wait for this man who'd shown such promise began to wane. My habitual cynicism, mellowed by my ten-day retreat, resurfaced. My peace-is-in-the present-moment stupor lifted. I heard my every unmindful footstep grate upon the white stone pathways like fingernails on a chalkboard. I tried to walk as stealthily as a cat stalking its prey. I tried not to talk, not even to whisper, to other guests staying here during the retreat – a PhD candidate from NYU researching a giant Buddha statue, a Physics professor from Buenos Aires trying to re-calibrate his spiritual rhythm. I tried to meditate diligently and read books by Buddhism's hottest stars: Tenzin Palmo, Pema Chödrön, the Dalai Lama.

I tried not to read my guidebook. But I was drawn towards the Ajanta Caves, Mount Everest. "You could go and climb a Himalayan peak," the meditation leader from my retreat said when I asked about transportation options to the Nepal border. "Or you could stay here and climb your inner Himalayas."

She said this with such a matter-of-fact Dutch accent that I hid the *Lonely Planet* under the bed that evening, determined to overcome my desires. And then I received the letter.

It was passed to me in a red silk bag emblazoned with dragons and vines, the kind of bag Tibetans used to protect religious texts. It was passed to me like a relay-race baton, from behind, just when I was trying to focus on my footsteps while walking to my hut. The retreatants were already in the *gompa*. Not a word was spoken. Not a finger brushed. I took the baton without looking back, and ran.

It was a love letter. Even though we'd only spent two nights together in a mosquito-infested hotel room that smelled of Dettol, the Italian claimed to love me. I was Angelina now. I was not just *bellissima*; I was the most *bellissima*. The letter continued, growing more and more sentimental. Suddenly I felt overwhelmed by all this business. I'd heard these words before, in various accents, and I'd lost faith in their power to create happiness.

Finally, at this retreat centre, I was beginning to discover why. Life is suffering. The evidence was everywhere: the emaciated gardener and his patched trousers; the rickshaw cyclist driver waiting by the front gate with his too-big sandals that kept missing the pedals; the mange-covered dogs whimpering in their sleep. But I was learning there were other less obvious forms of suffering. The constant little ache in my right shoulder I wished would go away. The feeling of annoyance towards the South American professor when he complained about paying fifty cents for a five-kilometre rickshaw ride. The longing for an ice-cold drink in a place where an ice cube was as luxurious as a white truffle. That kind of suffering. The suffering of wanting, of expecting. The trick, I was beginning to learn, was to stop. Stop wanting. Expecting. To train my mind to be content.

I didn't expect the flowers. A marigold blossom deposited silently by the side of my plate as I ate papaya. A full-blown rose resting in the arch of my flip-flop outside the hut. And then came the touches. The brief touch on my lower back that set off shivers as I stirred honey into my tea. The slow fan of fingers across my shoulders as I stacked dinner plates. Soon he began to look at me. When the spiritual director wasn't about and the other retreatants were busy contemplating the ground, he looked at me with eyes blazing like he knew all about this suffering business. But despite it all, he'd chosen to love.

Finally, after three weeks of silence, I let go. I let go of not wanting to fall in love and fell in love. I fell in love with the way he walked. The way he held his fork. The way he bowed to pet the goats. The way he always let others go ahead of him in the food line. I fell in love with loving. What else was there to do?

It was only natural then that we bumped into one another on the *gompa* rooftop after everyone had gone to bed. The sky at that time of night was too filled with stars to be wasted. The surrounding rice paddies too filled with the song of chirping insects. It was cool enough to ward off mosquitoes, cool enough that we had to hold one another to keep warm. It was on the rooftop that he whispered, "*Ti amo*," and talked of us living together in Naples.

I let go. I let myself dream of geraniums on the sill and a lanky, tri-coloured cat. Maybe we were just two people trying to alleviate just a little bit of suffering in this world. One person at a time. Maybe it was enough to be silent.

THE GARDENER

THEY STOOD WITH THEIR EYES FOCUSED on the place in front of them. A speck on the flagstones. A blade of grass. A right foot rose. Descended. Heel, then arch, then toe. A left foot rose. After ten steps, they stopped and stood still, as though trying to remember something important. Then they turned, raised a foot, and began again. The retreatants walked like this several times a day for intervals of forty-five minutes, sometimes an hour. It depended on when Venerable Antonio, a Buddhist monk from Sardinia who oversaw the retreatants from the balcony of his room, decided to ring the bell.

Some walked even more slowly than others. One woman's movements were barely perceptible. It was almost feline, this awareness of movement, this concentration of energy and grace. The gardener watched the same woman from his place in the flower beds. He watched her golden hair shimmer past her hips.

The gardener looked confused by all of this. Confused in a country where it was common to pour pints of milk on the heads of bull deities, to chew a nut that caused teeth to turn red, to smear one's naked body in ash and dung. He cocked his head to one side, tucking grey hairs into a faded pink cloth he'd fashioned into a turban to block the sun. Perhaps he found it difficult to understand why anyone would choose to spend hours walking back and forth and not going anywhere. Especially someone rich enough to pay five times his daily wage to stay for one night at this centre.

I wish I could have explained they were trying to learn how to live in the present moment. At least that's what I'd heard Venerable Antonio preach from his balcony: "Feel the contact with the Earth. Feel each moment."

But I suspected the gardener knew more about the moment than anyone. I'd watched him cradling dahlia blossoms in his hands, smiling at their petals. I'd watched him staring up at the clear blue sky, seeming to read patterns in the scattering of molecules. "Boom!" he'd exclaimed across the garden that morning, paying no heed to the "Silence Please" signs posted on the tree trunks. "Boom!" he'd clapped his hands and looked at me with a huge one-toothed grin as I sat at my place beneath the *pipal* trees. A thunderstorm was on its way.

We watched the retreatants, the gardener and I, until the bell rang and they returned to the meditation hall. I returned to perusing my guidebook, to analyzing train schedules and budget hotels. The gardener walked barefoot through the flowerbeds, deadheading calendulas, pruning stray branches. He examined the branches of the tree beside my guest hut through too-large eyeglasses that hung crookedly on his face. He held the lenses straight to examine the bark. He caught me watching and smiled widely. "*Kerda* tree!" he yelled across the garden. "My wife makes good pickle!"

A package wrapped neatly in newspaper sat on the windowsill of my hut the next morning. A daub of bright orange *kerda* pickle rested inside. A fiery, bitter sensation filled my mouth the moment I tasted it. But the fire mellowed and the bitterness sweetened as I pulled back my curtains to watch the retreatants settle at tables in the garden. It was time for their breakfast. They sipped tea. Slowly. Some looked up at the clouds lingering after last night's storm. Some watched the fountain splash at the foot of a stone Buddha. A bald-headed man chewed slices of papaya. Slowly.

Even after everyone disappeared into the meditation hall and I settled at a table in the garden, the sweet aftertaste of the pickle lingered. I chewed my Tibetan bread as the gardener fished dead leaves out of the lotus pond. "Thank you!" I called and he looked up, holding his glasses straight until he recognized me.

"You like?" he yelled.

"I love!"

The bell rang. I closed my guidebook. The retreatants exited the hall to begin their slow march to the present moment. The gardener nodded, focusing his lenses where I was looking. The bald-headed man straightened his shoulders, the serene expression on his face illuminated by the sun. Even from here, I could see his long lashes and soft curve of lips. A right foot rose. Descended. Slowly, he moved toward my place beneath the *pipal* trees. I sensed the gardener luring him closer and closer. I waited for the bald-headed man to lift his gaze, to look at me, to walk through the grass until he reached my side. But he stopped, stood still for a moment, and turned.

THE WOMAN IN WHITE

Blankets off. Bare feet on cold cement. It was too early for the chatter of the Indian women sharing the corner room. Even the two perky Japanese volunteers in charge of the female dorms were still sleeping. Before India I never would have woken at such an early hour on purpose. Though it was tempting to stay in bed and gaze at the unadorned lavender-coloured walls and listen to the bells of the Hindu temple in the distance. But I'd been told the gods roamed the ether and fell to the earth with the morning dew between four and six o'clock in the morning. And I needed to brush my teeth and wash my face before the line-up began at the lone sink in the communal bathroom. Besides, the Japanese girls would come and find me if I stayed in bed. They hadn't taken a vow of silence and had no qualms about banging on doors, yelling "Wake up! Wake up!" and personally escorting anyone who slept in to their cushion in the meditation hall.

The deal was that if you were going to stay at Dhamma Bodhi for free – payment was made on a voluntary basis at the end of the retreat – you had better follow the schedule. S.N. Goenka, founder of this meditation centre and dozens of others throughout the world, didn't want lack of finances to prevent anyone from participating. Once a successful businessman who suffered from migraines and depression, Goenka claims he was saved by Vipassana, a mediation technique taught by the Buddha 2,500 years ago. The technique is science, he says. Pure science. I had learned all this every evening from seven o'clock to quarter past eight when we were expected to watch Goenka's videotaped lectures, featuring the merry and rather chubby guru sitting cross-legged and talking into the camera. Sometimes his wife, who was also on the portly side, made a special appearance, joining in for mantra chanting, or just sitting there, meditating, while her husband laughed about our out-of-control "monkey minds."

Today was Day Three. The days of the week didn't exist at Dhamma Bodhi. It was a countdown. When I signed up for Goenka's ten days of meditation in the countryside of Bihar to pass time while Giuseppe was meditating a few kilometres away at Root Institute, it had all sounded so pleasant. Indian food. Private room overlooking a courtyard. The centre was surrounded by "long stretches of fertile agricultural fields" where lentils, wheat, and potatoes flourished. Beyond the fields snaked the Phalgu River, where none other than the Buddha himself had walked alongside its banks on his path to enlightenment.

I had arranged for a rickshaw to the centre's gates and entered the whitewashed compound on foot. Even though the bustling town of Bodh Gaya was so close by, the centre felt isolated. Behind the front gates, the golden spires of a pagoda rose from a barren-looking acreage. "Passport," the man at the check-in office commanded. He looked soldier-like with his crew cut and starched white shirt. I'd been wary about relinquishing my passport, but he assured me it would be kept in a safe along with all my other valuables. He asked for books, notepads, writing implements, confiscating anything that might distract me from observing "the changing nature of body and mind." The dusty road leading back to Bodh Gaya had looked tempting then. But my rickshaw driver had already left.

I looked up at the square of starry sky in the courtyard and headed to the bathroom. I brushed my teeth in the sparkling white sink, cleaned several times a day by the Japanese volunteers. No mirrors. Cold water only, except for one hour of hot in the evening, when we signed up to take showers. Signs warned that washing clothes was prohibited. But the Indian women ignored this rule. Every day they scrubbed their saris in basins of the forbidden hot water on their hands and knees. They wrung them out on the bathroom floor and hung them in the courtyard to dry. "Please read sign. Read sign!" the Japanese girls pleaded.

The Indian women shrugged. "No English," they said, standing in puddles of water.

I splashed cold water on my face and massaged Himalaya Herbals facewash (one of the few items not confiscated from my backpack) around in circles.

Day Three. For the first two days we'd sat on our cushions and watched our breath. To be more specific, we'd tried to feel the air coming in and out of our nostrils. We weren't supposed to fidget or fall asleep while doing this for more than ten hours a day. A volunteer was always watching and didn't hesitate to give you a poke, or even a shove, and tell you to leave if you couldn't cut it. On Day One I'd secretly hoped to be ordered back to my dorm where the chatter of the Japanese girls would have been a welcome distraction from my nostrils.

The final gong sounded, telling us it was time to make our way to the meditation hall for Day Three's morning mantra chanting. But I was already there, sitting on the marble steps waiting for the doors to open. Dark forms emerged from the shadows, draped in the ubiquitous shawls of India. I pulled my imitation pashmina shawl from Varanasi closer. "Real, yes, very real," the shopkeeper had assured me. Woodsmoke from the village beyond the perimeter of the centre's fence laced the air. As the other western women arrived – the men entered by a different door – I felt their camaraderie even though it was forbidden to say good morning or exchange other pleasantries. All of us had chosen to be here, in this country, at this hour, with a day of breathing on a cushion ahead of us. The strength of our silence grew as we stared into our own squares of sky or withered garden. And then the Indian ladies arrived. One by one, they tried to break us, engaging us in conversation. "Where are you from?" "Is your husband here?" I tried to look away from their kohl-lined eyes and nose rings, to look down. But they were so filled with good cheer and enthusiasm. So happy to be alive at such an early hour.

The Japanese girls had been impotent in their attempts to silence them. Instead, they had taken to talking to the Indian ladies in low, furtive whispers. In the pale-blue glow of the meditation hall, their chatter turned into bangle jangling, farting, belching, sari rustling. Every morning they waved at their husbands across the gender divide in the centre of the room, sometimes even calling out their names. The men ignored them.

Our ranks had become divided. The Indians and the westerners. Nowhere had this become more evident than at breakfast. The Indian women were always first in line. The cooks watched helplessly as they piled their stainless-steel plates with so much food the partitions disappeared. The westerners watched helplessly from the back of the line. Did they think what I was thinking? Will there be anything left for me? Are the Indian women using this retreat to gorge themselves? But who would sit through so many hours of observing their nostrils just for a free bowl of *dal* and rice?

I drew my shawl closer, wishing they'd open the meditation hall doors. The Indian women asked: "Is your country this cold?" "Do you really live in igloos?" Then the woman in white emerged from one of the private cottages, her hair covered, her head bent low. I couldn't tell if she was a westerner or Indian. But it didn't matter. The moment she appeared, the Indian women went silent. The woman in white glided along like a ghost, hands clasped behind her back. The door of the meditation hall opened as her bare foot touched its threshold, as if on cue. "They say this is her sixtieth retreat," one of the Indian women whispered. "I am only at five. We are so fortunate to be in the presence of such wisdom."

THE RICKSHAW CYCLIST

IT WAS TWO O'CLOCK IN the afternoon. "How far is it to Lumbini?" I asked a rickshaw cyclist in front of the newsstand.

"Twenty-eight kilometres," he answered.

Everyone within hearing distance bobbed their heads up and down.

"Yes, yes, twenty-eight," the shoe repair man confirmed.

"Will you take me there?"

For a moment, the rickshaw cyclist looked surprised. He looked towards the Indian border guard who had just stamped an exit visa in my passport. His eyes narrowed. "One thousand rupees. Indian rupees."

He knew I had no other option. There was a nation-wide strike today and he was my only chance to escape this border town with too many bored-looking men loitering about.

I didn't haggle. I nodded and climbed onto the vinyl-covered double-seat on wheels, welded by iron bars to his bicycle. I propped my feet onto my backpack. He made a move to pull the parasol over my head.

"That's okay," I said. "I want to feel the breeze," I said. But really I wanted to be able to turn and say good-bye to India. My six-month tourist visa was due to expire the next day, just when I was getting to know "Mother India." The next time I'd see her would be when I flew from Kathmandu to Delhi a month later. And then I would only see her from inside Indira Gandhi International Airport as I transited back to the west.

The rickshaw cyclist mounted the bicycle and waved to his friends. They started yelling in Hindi – asking him where he was going, I imagined, and for how much. But he didn't answer.

He pushed hard on the pedals and we accelerated, cruising through the streets, past the last bored man in front of the butcher shop, the last cinder block shack.

The rickshaw cyclist stood up, pedalling away at maximum force. We rode in the middle of the road, the breeze full in our faces. He turned around and smiled. I noticed the sun still high in the sky, the sweat soaking his armpits. "Would you like to stop for some water?" I asked, pointing to a drink stand up ahead. He shook his head, and pedalled even harder.

The roads were empty. A few lone cyclists passed, laden with canned goods, containers of water, car parts propped onto their carriers. For once, the countryside unfurled quietly, slowly. Barren fields transformed into carpets of green rice plants and yellow mustard. We pedalled beneath the branches of *bodhi* trees, past conical mounds of harvested grain. Past soft curves of adobe huts with thatched roofs.

Children ran onto the road, screeching, laughing, mimicking the rickshaw cyclist's strained expression and my repose. I knew in my gut there was something wrong about all this. Some travellers refused to travel by cycle-rickshaw.

But the rickshaw cyclist laughed along. He turned and waved as we crossed a bridge and rounded a bend.

We stopped where pyramids of oranges, grapes, guavas and pomegranates were stacked on a cart. He pointed to a bunch of bananas hanging from a hook and pulled a crumpled bill from his pocket, handing it to the vendor. He kept one small banana and passed the rest to me. "Eat," he said, and began to pedal again, peeling the banana as he rode. Next he stopped to buy homemade popsicles out of a foam cooler. I offered him rupees, but he shook his head and mounted his seat. We ate the popsicles quickly, drips flying behind us as he pedalled.

In two hours we reached Lumbini. The town looked deserted. "Where?" he asked, coasting along the main street. I'd thought about this question, had consulted the pages of the *Lonely Planet* while he bought bags of peanuts in the last town.

"The Korean Monastery," I answered. I'd read of its clean rooms and *kimchi*. He stopped and asked two men standing outside the telephone office for directions. The men talked loudly and gesticulated. They stared at me like hungry wolves. I stared straight ahead, as I'd learned from the women of India. I sat very erect to let them know they shouldn't mess with the likes of me.

"No good town," the rickshaw cyclist said. "Nepalis, no good people."

As we entered the gates of the temple complex and its monasteries, I began to feel more uneasy. The rickshaw cyclist stopped, asking the gatekeeper directions. The man gestured towards the forest, then asked, "Are you alone?"

It was too late to turn back. We'd come too far. Besides, this was the birthplace of the Buddha. A holy place. No one would take such chances with their karma, would they?

We cycled along a gravel footpath beside an artificial lake. Two swans glided past. "Please keep off," read hand-painted signs on a vast expanse of dead grass labelled "Peace Park."

Beyond the grass, the forest began, and we turned down another, narrower gravel path. I imagined the Buddha walking among these trees. Talking to the birds. Amused by the map of international monasteries that had sprung up beside the creek: Thailand, Germany, Vietnam, Burma. Ornate-looking domes and construction cranes poked out of the forest canopy.

We spotted Korea on the map and crossed a wooden bridge. Our tires fishtailed in the gravel. The rickshaw cyclist strained at the pedals, his straight back finally beginning to slump. I was about to offer to walk the rest of the way, but then an enormous structure the colour of wet cement appeared on the horizon – a three-tiered pagoda-like temple with bamboo scaffolding crisscrossing its outer walls. We arrived at the black wrought-iron gate of the Korean monastery. The rickshaw cyclist rang the buzzer. A man in a grey cotton pantsuit peered out of a building inside the gates and looked at me. The gates swung open.

I dismounted, and the rickshaw cyclist began to follow me. But the man in the grey pantsuit held up his palm, shooing him back onto the gravel. The cyclist disobeyed. He left his rickshaw and entered the monastery. We gawked at the enormous unfinished temple before us, the men perched on the scaffolding, the sound of drilling echoing through the chambers. I took him aside, pushed the bills into his hand – twice the price we'd negotiated.

He stuffed the bills into his pocket and thanked me with his eyes downcast. "No good place," he said. He looked at the man in the pantsuit who still hadn't smiled. "I bring you back to India?" he offered.

I watched as he mounted the bicycle and pedalled off into the late afternoon light. He turned and waved as he rounded the corner.

part three

BETWEEN THE PLANKS

THERE IS A GAP BETWEEN here and there, between a dust-filled street in a dusty subcontinent, and a cedar plank cottage in a west coast rainforest. A gap unchinked by hours of buses, planes, boats, by all those litres of fuel, evaporated. It all trails behind me, clunking along like a string of tin cans on a newlyweds' car – all those bodies of water, swaths of land, and this plank of western red cedar. I run my hand along its grain, remembering the faces – airport officials, ticket sellers, chai vendors, and that little boy standing by a pile of garbage on the side of the road where the buses pulled in, holding up torn trousers with one hand – all that suffering bunched up in his palm. The bus drove away. The plane took off. The boat sailed. And there is a gap between here and there. I can feel it blowing between the planks – cool as a northwest wind in a west coast rainforest.

THE ITALIAN DOGGY

HE TOLD ME HE WANTED to be my little Italian doggy and follow me everywhere. That was before Haida Gwaii. Fifty-three degrees north, one hundred thirty-two degrees west—formerly known as the Queen Charlotte Islands, or, as the locals called it, the edge of the world. It was the kind of place that escaped Ice Ages, where endemic species such as kinnikinnick and giant black bears flourished. It was home to Sasquatch trackers, German opera singers, dope dealers, Tartar goat herders, Greenpeace activists, and an Indigenous people once known as the Vikings of the Northwest Coast.

It took a while to arrive at the edge of the world. Especially if you began in Kathmandu. It had been there, on the rooftop of the Tibet Peace Guest House, that Giuseppe and I looked for Everest and saw nothing but the polluted haze of the Kathmandu Valley. Our eyes had begun to smart. "I know a place with the freshest air in the world." I had said.

We were freshly in love then. We spent our days eating *momos* and drinking pots of Nepali spice tea on the single bed of Room 204. An Italian jazz musician and a Canadian poet – *poetessa*, as Giuseppe was fond of saying. Two days remained before he was due to fly back to Italy. We had yet to mention the f-word. The future was challenging at the best of times, but even more so when people of two different nationalities met abroad. Especially two people with Fine Arts degrees who still stored their belongings at their parents' homes and had no imminent job prospects.

Giuseppe wanted to know more about the fresh air. I told him of a land of white sand beaches, sparkly blue waters, and emerald-hued forests. "People don't even lock their doors," I said. Poetry in the dunes. Wild strawberries, huckleberries, sea asparagus. "People just leave their keys in the ignition." The sound of the surf, of rain on the roof.

We stopped en route in Vigevano, Italy, to visit his family. There we slept beneath hand-embroidered sheets and walked upon white marble floors. His mother ironed handkerchiefs of the finest Italian linen for Giuseppe's upcoming voyage. I should have warned him then.

I should have warned him about the cabin awaiting us at the edge of the world – a cabin named "The Empress." It was one of several off-the-grid cabins that comprised Rapid Richie's Rustic Rentals Reasonable Rates (otherwise known as Rrrrr!). I should have explained "off the grid" meant no running water or electricity. An outhouse. A Coleman cooler for a fridge. It meant wool socks and jeans and getting dirty. It meant crouching in a blue plastic tote and having someone pour tepid water down your back to get clean. Those were the days before this lifestyle choice acquired a sort of glamour, and became the stuff of reality TV shows and the dream of inner-city hipsters.

By then I'd learned Giuseppe had trained at conservatories bearing the names of famous Italian composers. He'd worked at the music library of La Scala. He'd played gigs with the likes of Lee Konitz and Bob Mintzer. But I'd also learned he'd never done typical Canadian activities, like ice skate, or camp.

"Do you like to camp?" I asked.

"Camp?"

"You know, sleep outside in a tent."

"Why would anyone want to sleep outside when they can sleep inside?"

Giuseppe worried about things like damaging his hands. His fingers were like ten golden ingots, each a precious tool to press a key of his beloved sax. When his father asked him to prune the rose arbour, I could see him wince in anticipation of potential damage. The skin on his hands was as soft and unlined as kid gloves.

We strolled through Vigevano's *Piazza* Ducale – an ornate affair of frescoes and archways that Leonardo da Vinci helped design. Giuseppe pointed to a short black skirt in the window of one of the posh boutiques lining the perimeter.

"That would suit you, with a nice pair of high heels," he said.

If only he'd known I was the kind of girl more suited to rubber boots. But I dared not tell him that back then. I watched the Italian women strut past, and admired their blood-red lipstick and put-together look that could only come from centuries of advanced civilization. In Piazza Ducale I suddenly figured out what I really wanted to be – Italian.

Giuseppe's mother wanted me to be Italian too. I could tell she was puzzled by her son's choice of mates – the sunburned nose, the mousy hair, the sandals in April, the wardrobe I'd acquired after seven months of travelling in Nepal and India: long flowing tunics of colourful cottons.

She took my measurements and began to sew a summer dress for me to wear at the edge of the world. A dress of sheer cream silk with camel-coloured polka-dots.

Giuseppe and I strolled arm-in-arm amongst the chestnut trees on the grounds of Castello Sforzesco, eating gelato. Policemen rode past on shiny bicycles with fenders. I'd begun to think we should stay here forever, but Giuseppe was keener than ever to see the edge of the world. He couldn't wait to swim in the sparkly blue waters. I didn't have the heart to tell him that the temperature of such waters rarely breached ten degrees Celsius. Instead, I allowed Giuseppe's illusions to fester. I allowed him to pack the white linen chinos, the Renato Balestra shirt, the black Speedo.

And then one day – after thirteen hours of planes, eight hours of buses, and thirty-one hours of ferries – we finally reached the edge of the world. Once upon a time I'd thought taking the long way was the only way to go. That it gave me a better perspective of the geographies traversed, and time to adjust to new surroundings. But now I knew taking the long way meant spending the night at a youth hostel filled with drunken nineteen-year-old Australians, searching for a bus station at six in the morning while pulling an oversized Italian suitcase uphill in a town that stinks of pulp mill, sleeping on the puce-coloured carpet of the Raven deck with the Haida Bucks basketball team on board a ferry, walking five kilometres along train tracks in the rain to find a sandwich. Taking the long way meant the loyalty of your Italian doggy might wane. And the culinary delights of BC Ferries' Canoe Cafe would do little to revive him.

"What's that?" Giuseppe asked.

"Vinegar. Don't you like vinegar on your fries?"

Giuseppe looked out at the dark seas swelling around us. Tonight we were due to cross the Hecate Strait – the fourth-most-dangerous body of water in the world.

"Just another eight hours," I said, digging into the fries.

It was six in the morning when we finally saw land. Giuseppe wondered about the bus to our next and final destination.

"There's no bus on the island," I said.

"Taxi?"

It began to rain, of course.

"We'll have to hitchhike," I said.

"What?"

"You know, stick out our thumbs and get a ride with someone else."

"I know what hitchhike means. No."

"No?"

"I will not hitchhike."

I should have felt compassion by then. My doggy had black rings under his eyes. One of the wheels of his suitcase had broken off. But maybe I wanted to test his mettle.

"There's no choice," I said.

"I'll walk."

"It'll take days."

"I'll walk."

It was our first real argument.

"We could rent a car but it will be very expensive," I said.

"Good."

"It's probably not open yet. We'll have to wait."

"I don't care."

He seemed happier once we were driving the red jeep up-island. At that point, we still had our tans from India, and memories of warmth. We sang silly songs and drove further into the north.

Finally, tarmac turned to gravel and we drove through a tunnel of conifers, veering away from the potholes. The forest thinned to a scraggly stand of Sitka spruce and stagnant ponds. A sign: "Rapid Richie's Rustic Rentals Reasonable Rates. Rrrrrr!" We drove up Lupine Lane and parked in the sandy parking lot.

"We're here!" I stood and breathed in the fresh air.

Giuseppe sat in the jeep, shivering.

"Wait until you see the beach. It's just a few minutes down that path," I said.

Silence.

"Why don't we go get the key to the cabin?" I asked.

When we opened the blue door of The Empress, it became even more obvious I'd made a mistake. Last season's mess greeted us. Plates caked with spaghetti sauce filled the makeshift sink. Sand, dead leaves, crushed crab shells on the plywood floor.

"What's that?" Giuseppe pointed to the bed. At first I thought he meant the futon, the tangle of polyester sheets. But then I saw the telltale scattering of chocolate brown, like cake sprinkles.

"It's mouse poo," I said.

The poo was scattered throughout the drawers where his fine Italian handkerchiefs would lie, on the counters where the Sicilian pecorino would be sliced. It was everywhere.

"That's it," he said.

By now I could only wonder why it had taken him so long to conclude he'd arrived in a country of barbarians, and that I, despite my charms in Tibet Peace Guest House's Room 204, was one of them.

"This is unacceptable. No Italian would accept this," he said.

I waited for him to get back into the jeep and drive into the waning light. But he didn't. He opened his suitcase. He extracted a set of his mother's hand-embroidered sheets, snapping them expertly above the futon. I swept up the mouse poo. He boiled pots of water. We cleaned until the frogs began to sing.

NOTES FROM OFF THE GRID

1. The Road

FIRST A SIGN: "Proceed with Caution: Narrow, Winding Road." The forest thickens. Cedars creep back to the edge. Moss grows in mufflers, hangs in gossamer veils. Tamped pathways rusty with leaf mulch all lead towards the Pacific. Cabins built of driftwood and salvaged glass. People who chop wood, collect rainwater in barrels. They light candles or propane lanterns, tune to CBC on battery-operated radio. Or they listen to silence.

2. Silence

IT HAS A SOUND, a fullness. Heavy with sigh of tree, and space between breath. Ripe with pause between birdsong and crash of surf. No one tells us it's addictive. The ear seeks it as a musician's seeks a Bach "Partita" or an Ellington "Suite." We crave its harmonious overtures, and well-timed rests. Crunch of foot on leaves. Knock on wooden door. Creak of rusty hinge. Steaming kettle and clanking teacup, rat-a-tat-tat of conversation. This is why – we think, all the while holding up our end of the conversation – this is why people become hermits.

3. Conversation

IT'S ABOUT FIREWOOD – too wet, too knotty. About driving past Rose Spit, all the way to East Beach, chainsaw ready for bucking logs washed up from the world. Yellow cedar, mahogany, even yew. It's about storm reports from Thailand, catching waves that have travelled thousands of miles. Huckleberries ready to pick, salal berries ripening soon. Staying up all night canning coho, or pickling sea asparagus, or bottling elderflower wine. It's about the price of gas, the size of engines, the durability of tires (on these roads). Freight charges and air mail, Okanagan peaches five times the price. It's about Shauna pregnant for the first time, Estrella for the third. Everyone seems to be having babies. "Careful of the water," they say.

4. Water

WE COLLECT IT IN BLUE plastic eighty-four-litre garbage pails. It hits cedar shingles, drips into a trough, runs in a thin, steady stream. It's the colour of pale urine. They say it softens skin, brightens eyes. We boil it. Drink Earl Grey, rooibos, apple-cinnamon. We bathe in a basin just big enough to crouch. Wash each other's backs, feel it trickle down our spines, penetrate membranes. We feel it seep into those parts of ourselves we never knew existed.

AT THE EMPRESS

WE DANCE IN SILENCE ACROSS plywood. We sleep to the sound of singing frogs and a wind blowing from Alaska. We walk amongst sea stars, moon snails and empty shells of Dungeness. We imprint ourselves here, every day, in the wet sand, and every day we disappear.

LOOKING FOR THE FOREST

SOME COUPLES HAVE MAKE-UP SEX. Others bake. The other night, Giuseppe asked if I'd like to bake some coconut "macaronis." Even though it was only eight o'clock I was already in bed, and had been there for three hours, feigning sleep. I lay there angry about something Giuseppe had done or said; I couldn't remember what.

"Macaronis?" I asked. Giuseppe held the *Joy of Cooking* to the light. For the first time that day, I smiled.

"We're just missing a couple of ingredients," he said with his charming accent. It turned out we were missing two out of the four ingredients that go into making coconut macaroons. Like most angry people, I didn't really want to be angry. The "macaronis" were a perfect excuse to get out of bed.

"Let's go to the bakery," I suggested.

Luckily, we lived within a few minutes' walk from The Moon Over Naikoon bakery. The bakery and I had a tacit agreement. When it needed ground ginger or an onion, I retrieved these items from our cabin. When I needed a teaspoon of vanilla or an egg white, the bakery's sliding glass doors slid magically open and all was well.

The moon truly shone over Naikoon Provincial Park as we navigated our way along the dark forest path. At the top of the hill leading down to the bakery, Giuseppe shone his flashlight up into the trees. I stopped. "Wait," I said, craning my neck to see the tops of the spruce crowns. But they soared higher than the beam could reach. All around us tall dark forms reached up into the night, branches touching stars. In that moment, I remembered we lived in a forest. A magnificent 179,500 acre forest.

Had I turned into one of those people who couldn't see the forest for the trees? You'd think a place of such grand dimensions would inspire me to embrace the bigger picture. But what if you had no idea what the bigger picture was? Then you baked macaroons.

The macaroons wouldn't stick together at first. But we managed to plop them onto the baking tray and they managed to come out looking somewhat edible. Of course, it didn't matter. We were laughing again. At nothing. At everything.

TUESDAY, NORTH BEACH

THERE ARE MOUNTAINS HERE, riverbeds, glaciers, forest floors. Here, in a handful of stones. Obsidian, agate, red jasper. Geographies worn to their essence. We collect things: the spinal discs of whales, sea lion skulls, kestrel vertebrae. I suppose we think they're beautiful. They line our sills – sun-bleached, salt-leached, fragments of death. We admire their contours, the honed grace of it all. Caress cavities where a heart once lay.

THE PRINCESS AND THE POET

THERE'S A STORY ABOUT A PRINCE who grew up in an opulent setting in the foothills of the Himalayas. The prince married a beautiful princess and they loved one another deeply. But the day came when the prince grew disenchanted by wealth and earthly pleasures, and yearned to wander the tiger-infested jungles in search of the true meaning of existence.

The princess was saddened by the prince's news. Nevertheless, on the eve of his secret escape from the castle, she arranged for a horse to be saddled, his travelling cloak to be laid out, and a basket to be filled with provisions. She pretended to be asleep when he woke in the middle of the night, donned his cloak, and touched her cheek for one last time. She didn't want him to see her tears. And his story continues. Without the princess. But she is still there, lying on the silk sheets, listening for the hoof beats. She is wishing she won't have to wake in the morning and drink *chai* alone on the terrace where they had always sat together watching the sun rise above the castle walls.

Such stories repeated themselves. More than 2,500 years passed. The prince was a jazz musician, the princess, a poet. They lived in a two-room cedar-plank cabin on a remote island, nearly two hundred kilometres by ferry from the mainland of British Columbia, surrounded by temperate rainforest and the sound of frogs singing after dusk. The poet had just returned from an eight-hour waitressing shift at the Trout House Café. The musician was sitting on the couch in the dark with a fluffy tortoiseshell cat on his lap. The poet lit a few candles. Immediately, she knew something was wrong. The saxophone had been packed away in its case. The compositions were stacked neatly on top of the desk. The musician's eyes were red, as though he'd been crying. "I can't do it anymore," he said.

"What?" she asked, and for a moment she thought he was talking about music. About a tricky rhythm, a catchy melody.

"This," he said, and swept his hand across the cabin until it rested on her. "It's not me. I'm not meant for this kind of life."

She knew how the story went. She knew all about disenchantment and disillusionment. How could she write without them? She even knew that this day was inevitable. She'd met him in Bodh Gaya, after all – one of the holiest Buddhist pilgrimage sites in the world. At first she'd thought he was a monk with his shaved head, ultra-bright eyes, and the way he'd paid such close attention to everything she said. "Where are your robes?" she'd asked. "I'm too Italian to be a monk," he'd laughed.

The poet and the musician. The Canadian and the Italian. The atheist and the Buddhist. She should have known it would only be a matter of time – but we can't skip from the beginning of a story to its end. There was a middle part to be lived: the rising action, the climax.

"I want to become a monk," he said, stroking the cat's head. The poet struggled to stay calm. She'd been practicing for six months: breathing deeply, walking slowly, paying attention to the moment. But she felt vulnerable right now. Her feet were aching, and she was slightly grumpy from dealing with fickle customers. "It has nothing to do with you," he said, and some wild creature took over the poet, sucking her into its vortex. The cat jumped off the musician's lap and meowed to be let out. Couldn't he see that it had everything to do with her? That she would be the one left lying on the silk sheets, listening to hoof beats? Her mind rushed ahead to the dénouement – to the days ahead where they would unravel everything, disassemble their union. Pack boxes. Book flights. Oh yes, she knew the story well, knew it by heart.

She tried to smile despite the fact she wanted to run screeching into the icy Pacific. She tried to smile despite the fact she felt angry, betrayed – they were the musician and the poet, they were supposed to live in Naples, line their windowsills with geraniums and create great works of art. She tried to smile, to remember that she loved this man. Shouldn't she wish him happiness? But she couldn't smile; she couldn't even cry. She wished she could be more like the princess – saddle the horse, lay out his clothes, pack a basket.

And the story continued. The pair sat in their cedar-plank cabin and looked out at the trees. They were mostly silent. The cat purred. A week passed. A month. The dénouement continued without them. There were no angry outbursts. They held one another like never before. But soon, someone would have to take action. Soon a tourist visa would run out, a lease would expire.

It was the musician who broke first. "Why don't we move to Italy?"

he asked.

The poet should have said something then. She should have realized it was time to let go. Hadn't she met him in a place where the happiness of others was as entwined in your own wellbeing as the tiny, interconnecting veins of a leaf? But she didn't have enough faith. She feared being alone again. She thought she needed him upon this new path. Not to mention, she'd always wanted to live in Italy. "Let's go," she said.

THE HUMAN REALM

WE EXIST WHERE CATS SLEEP at the foot of beds and woodstoves glow with last night's embers. We have Earl Grey, rain on tin roofs, beaches swept by tides – a smell so fresh, so laced with life. And death, he tells me. He tells me to detach from the rise and fall of the cat's breath, from the taste of bergamot, from the raindrops pooled in starburst leaves glittering with sky. "It's all suffering," he says as I bend to touch my reflection. All suffering.

LA DOLCE VITA

THE JOURNEY BEGAN AT MASSET airport, where the daily flight departed at 11:20 a.m. and the locals checked in at 10:50. Security checks hadn't made it to these parts. The only precaution was to close the door leading to the tarmac. Airport staffers were more vigilant about things like wayward deer than terrorists. Just a few weeks ago, an incoming flight had hit a doe on the runway. The accident made the front page of *The Observer*, rallying the community to cull anything four-legged in the vicinity.

Two juice boxes and one packet of Dad's cookies later and we were in Vancouver. In just a few hours, we had gone from heating rainwater for our morning bath to eating French éclairs at Fratelli's. After a few days, we boarded a flight bound for Milan. In London-Gatwick, we waited eight hours for the final leg of our journey, eating edamame-watercress salad from Marks and Spencer while watching the world stream out of Arrivals.

After an airport shuttle, subway, and train, we walked towards Via Scapardini 9 where Giuseppe's family awaited. It was always during these jet-lagged, hazy moments that things become clearer. Not even a week had passed since we'd left our off-the-grid refuge, and I was drawn to the energy of the Italians like a moth to the light. I was drawn to the floodlit windows of *pasticcerie* piled high with creations of flour and sugar, to the *caffés*, to the sparkle of glasses against mirrored walls.

As we walked, the wheels of our luggage trolley joined in the cacophony. When we reached the Chiesa della Madonna del Carmine, I gazed up at the floodlit statue of the Madonna with her arms raised up into the night, and I realized, even though I hadn't slept for twenty-four hours, just how alive I felt.

The feeling continued. It continued through meal after meal of dishes curated by an Italian housewife. The sharpest pecorinos. The ripest persimmons. "*Mangia! Mangia!*" Giuseppe's father insisted. And I did. I ate. And I ate some more. I filled myself with the energy of a country fuelled by the quest for la *dolce vita*.

And it was in Venice where I truly found my *dolce vita*. A courtyard. A fountain. Houses fitting into one another. Geraniums spilling down thousand-year-old walls. A woman opening green-painted shutters to tilt her face towards the sun. I crossed tiny arched bridges and ducked through porticos. Drank a cappuccino beside a floating produce market. All along, I could have been doing this instead. I could have been hanging my laundry across a canal calling *"Buongiorno!"* to my neighbour. How could I ever have lived anywhere without marble tiles and frescoes? The Venetians managed all this splendour long before any sort of electrical grid had existed. Why is it I hadn't even managed to sew a pair of curtains?

Such questions lingered all the way back to Vigevano. They arose over and over while vineyards – and the place where Romeo met Juliet – flashed past the windows of the train. In this frame of mind, even the graffiti inspired me – *Ti amo tanto* (I love you so much), scrawled in black across white stucco. "I love you too," I felt like calling across the tracks.

SIGHTS UNSEEN

SOMETIMES, IF THE WINDOWS weren't too covered in graffiti, I could see the Alps from the train. And sometimes, if there wasn't too much smog, I could see them from the *Letteratura Americana* room at the library.

At main intersections, blue signs with white lettering pointed towards place-names that belonged in films with starlets wearing dark glasses and silk head scarves: Torino, Pavia, Alessandria. And just on the other side of the station beckoned a street called Corso Roma – the way to Rome.

But I sat there at Via Cairoli 4 – a studio apartment in Vigevano. And I was happy to sit there.

Travel guidebooks told me I should hike my way to happiness, gaze awestruck at the works of Tintoretto, wander along winding, cobblestone side streets dotted with *prosecco*-sipping locals.

But I was rather fond of the grocery store down the street. On most mornings its aisles were packed with seniors filling baskets with thinly sliced meats, *borlotti* beans and litres of red table wine. I liked the ladies who wore furs and heels at 9 a.m. I liked it when they asked me if I could reach the sparkling mineral water on the top shelves.

"*Grazie*," they said as I passed them a case. "*Grazie*," they said again, and I felt the thrill of an Italian word blooming in my mouth. "*Prego*," I said, louder than necessary.

I liked to watch the cashiers sitting on swivel chairs scanning purchases and joking about things I couldn't understand. I didn't really know why I liked these things so much – maybe I would have liked the Alps more. But I didn't think so.

Lately, it seemed that travelling was best done while sitting still. I didn't know when exactly I discovered this. Maybe it was in India after visiting one too many ancient temples that drew tourists, as the *Lonely Planet* described it, "like moths to a wondrous flame."

Maybe it was when I read somewhere that collecting experiences had become a western trend. I'd never been a trendsetter. But for the past eighteen years I'd been collecting experiences. I'd collected Varanasi, the Louvre. The Blarney Stone, the Sahara. Now I was sitting here at Via Cairoli 4, the splendour of the rest of Italy a mere train ticket away. And

I was content to go to the local *piazza*.

The *piazza* was large and bordered on all sides by arched walkways, *caffés* lit by chandeliers, Renaissance murals of birds and mermaids and vines, and copper drain-pipes shaped like dragons jutting from tiled rooftops.

I was the only tourist there. On weekdays from ten in the morning until noon, the cobblestones were dotted with trios of old men standing and talking. A policeman rode up and down the pathway through the *piazza's* centre on an old-fashioned bicycle with fenders and a horn. Everyone rode similar bicycles, the women's with baskets on the front.

The women wore pointy-toed boots, patterned tights, and miniskirts while riding. They wore scarves thrown over their shoulders and the right shade of lipstick. If it rained, everyone held colourful, grand-domed umbrellas aloft with one hand while steering with the other. I liked to watch these things while standing on stones laid in the pattern of radiating sunbeams.

I learned a lot by observing. I observed the produce vendors at the market examine radicchio for imperfections, trim artichokes, proffer segments of Sicilian clementines that still bore their leaves. "Very sweet," they promised, "very fresh."

I observed the couple at the mill scoop the perfect amount from bags filled with grains, rice, and nuts. I observed how the line-up snaked past the chicken feed. The couple remained calm trying to decode my Italian. The wife taught me how to say *mandorla* – almond. The husband heaved bags filled with soybeans and lentils into the centre of the room. "These are from your country," he said, opening the bags so I could see inside, the tiny beans and pulses running through his fingers.

It was a slower process than travelling, this observing, this sitting still. Sometimes it was even boring. At one o'clock in the afternoon, the streets of the town were empty. Everyone was at home eating. Everything was closed until four. Giuseppe was teaching music somewhere in Milan, every day, for twelve hours a day. And so it was just me left, sitting on a bench, and the pigeons cooing and pecking at things growing between the stones.

There was a kind of silence. The silence of people indoors, eating together as they'd done since before Rome existed. I thought of them at the table, pouring a glass of sparkling water. I thought of the women unzipping their boots and putting on slippers. I closed my eyes and imagined pulling out a chair and sitting down with them. I imagined how they would drizzle olive oil on the radicchio and encourage me to mangia, mangia. And I would sit there. Sit still. Let them collect me into their fold with a crusty roll ripped in two. A spoonful of lentils.

THIS IS SUNDAY LUNCH

LUNCHES WERE QUIET at Via Scapardini 9. Father. Mother. Son. And me, the girlfriend from Canada. We ate in the kitchen with the ticking of the clock, sometimes an Italian soap opera. We all had our places around the table. Mine was beside the radiator with my back to the television. I faced an armoire bursting with all manner of pot and platter, and kitchen appliances stored in their original boxes. I faced Giuseppe's mother.

I learned many things at my place beside the radiator. I learned that no matter how full I was I should always ask for seconds. If I didn't, they'd arrive on my plate anyway, and everyone was much happier if I'd asked for them first. "A good appetite!" the father would exclaim and beam in the direction of his son. I learned that bread sat directly on the tablecloth, pears were presented chilled and covered with water droplets, grapes were to be broken off in bunches, oranges peeled with a knife. I learned that cheese from Sicily, the region Giuseppe's family was originally from, was always best; "Sometimes Sardinia," the father may have said if he was feeling gracious.

I learned that even though I didn't normally drink coffee, I should drink one when all was said and done. I should down the thick, black espresso served in a tiny cup like a shooter. "It helps digestion," the mother said, stacking the cups the moment the last dregs were drunk. It was time to do the dishes. This was my cue to select a tea towel from the drawer. "No, not that one," the mother inevitably said as she filled the sink with soapy water. There were certain towels, I'd learned, for certain tasks – hand drying, glassware, pots. Although, in my opinion, they all looked exactly the same.

While I waited with the proper towel in hand and a mind buzzing with caffeine, the father prepared the leftovers for distribution to Bricciola, the family dog, and the flock of chickens. Nothing was wasted at Via Scapardini 9. Every fruit peel was minutely diced. Every cheese rind slivered. The father sat at the table while doing all this, big farmer's hands grasping a tiny pen-knife reserved just for this task. Leftover pasta was thrown into Bricciola's saucepan, topped with all the scrapings from our plates, and sprinkled with fresh Parmesan grated from a block half the size of my head.

When the father was finished, his son removed the tablecloth and carried it to the garden to shake out the crumbs. If I still didn't have a dish to dry, I went out too. I turned my face towards a sun that always seemed to be shining. I watched Giuseppe, knowing this had been his chore for thirty-one years. He shook out the tablecloth with a precise snap of his wrists. Crumbs settled gently on basil and arugula. He looked at me while folding the cloth into a perfect square. If no one was around, I clasped his hands where the corners met and kissed him.

This was Sunday lunch. It took me a while not to feel nervous every time we rounded the bend of our street and faced the statue of the Madonna rising into the blue sky. Her white marble form rising from the pinnacle of a pink-stuccoed church marked the entranceway to Via Scapardini. On a really clear day, the Alps a backdrop for her outstretched arms. Every time I rounded that bend I was reminded of two things: first, that Italy was beautiful; and second, that I was not Italian. I was a *straniero*, a stranger, a foreigner in the polite sense of the word.

This fact became evident every Sunday lunch. I didn't speak more than a few dozen words of the language, and these were mostly limited to what I saw on my plate. I didn't wear pointy boots with heels. I didn't know the names of the characters on *Vivere*.

Giuseppe assured me that none of this was important; his parents didn't care about such things. But I knew he was just being polite. Of course they cared; they were Italian. To make matters worse, they were Sicilian. They were from an island where traditionally *la famiglia* was worth killing for. And Giuseppe was their youngest. The one they'd been so patient with. The one they'd let study jazz in Boston, work as a musician on cruise ships, volunteer at a Buddhist retreat centre in India. He was their last chance for a four-hundred-guest wedding. For grandchildren.

I'd caught his mother examining my boots on the mat at the front door, scraping the toe with her pinkie nail to test if they were real leather. She had pulled me aside, examining the frayed stitching of a shirt collar, insisting I change while she mended it. She clucked when I walked barefoot through the garden. She sighed when I let Bricciola jump onto my lap, speckling my jeans with tiny paw-prints.

I knew they wondered why their son had chosen to bring home a scrawny, strawberry blonde with no fashion sense who had never eaten a fresh artichoke before. Sometimes, I wondered exactly the same thing. The longer I lived in this place, the more I wished I were Italian. Who wouldn't? They lived amidst carved cornices, soaring archways, and white marble staircases. They grew things like persimmons and passionfruit. They greeted one another with kisses on both cheeks and words that sounded like libretti. Mothers wearing stilettos pushed baby strollers. Every afternoon everything closed for three hours so people could eat a four-course lunch, then take a nap. And every week, after Sunday lunch, families walked arm-in-arm through the *piazza* beneath frescoes painted during the Renaissance.

But I learned that Giuseppe's family didn't go to the *piazza*. We sat back down at our places around the table and did what I dreaded most – talked. They asked questions. Giuseppe translated: "How many brothers do you have? What do they do? What does your father do? What does your family grow in their garden?" Giuseppe tried to find the words for nuclear power plant and car manufacturing industry. Retired school principal and mega-box chain store. "They don't have a garden?" the father asked, puzzled, looking at his son. I nodded, as saddened as he by this discovery. Soon they began to look at me with pity rather than disappointment. We downed another round of espressos. We cracked walnuts open and popped them into our mouths.

After a few weeks, when my vocabulary began to expand beyond the border of my plate, I asked: "Why did you leave Sicily?" I'd realized that although they'd lived in the North for almost 30 years, far from African breezes and lemon trees, Sicily was still home. Via Scapardini 9 was filled with all things Sicilian: sheep's ricotta, cannoli shells, olive oil, pistachios, a thick sweet wine called *Zibibbo*, reserved for special occasions. The wine was kept on a side rack in the fridge. Unlabelled.

"Don't drink it," Giuseppe warned when a glass was presented to me on All Saints' Day. But of course I'd learned to accept whatever was placed in front of me.

"*Salute!*" I said and took a sip. It tasted heavenly. "Ambrosia of the gods," I attempted to say while they all looked at me, confused.

"It's really strong," Giuseppe warned again as I took another sip. And it was. It made my head buzz in a way espresso could never dream of. The father smiled. I smiled back. I understood I was tasting where he came from. The essence of the place. The sweetness of sun, sea, wind, soil. I tasted what the North could never replace.

"Why did you leave?" I asked again. The mother opened the drawer where the tea towels were kept and unfolded a square of white linen printed with a map of Sicily. It was illustrated with orange blossoms, dancing peasant girls, Grecian urns. She pointed to a dot nestled in green hills, a centimetre away from the Mediterranean Sea.

"Boom!" she said. "Boom!"

"There was an earthquake," Giuseppe translated. "They lost everything. They had to move North where there was work."

The mother rushed into the dining room and returned with a vase that, before I moved to Italy, I would have considered tacky. It was curvy and ornate, hand-painted with the scene of a cypress and a white-washed villa. The sky was pink. The glaze, a pearly opalescence. The mother held the vase aloft by its golden handles. "Real gold," she said. "It's all that survived." I looked at the vase as the light shifted and everything – sky, cypress, villa – began to shimmer. I sensed all those years preserved beneath the glaze.

"Take it," the mother said placing the vase in front of me. For the first time I refused something I was offered at Via Scapardini 9. "Take it," she said again, looking at me, not at my clothing or shoes or hairstyle. And I looked at her too. Something in her eyes told me I'd been wrong all this time – I'd been family from the moment I took my seat beside the radiator even though I was a *straniero*. I'd been family, not because I was living with her son, but because this was Italy. This was Sunday lunch.

"Thank you," I said, touching the golden handles.

THE HYBRIDS

KATY LEANED OUT HER WINDOW again. The one overlooking the terrace. She opened it every time she heard me out there, anxious, I thought, to speak our mother tongue. "We're hybrids!" she yelled down. I pinned a T-shirt onto the clothesline, taking a second to admire the medieval castle wall jutting up into the blue sky, then turned, craning my neck to look up at her. She was wearing curlers in her hair and a white silk nightgown. French silk, she'd told me on another occasion. "We're hybrids," she repeated, winding a stray tendril of grey. "There's no escaping it."

Katy from New Zealand and Angela from Canada. Passports made it sound so simple. But Katy was right. We were hybrids. Our friends used pencil to record our latest address. We shape-shifted to fit the demands of the day – scarves draped to hide hair, or tossed around necks into French twists. We lived in Cairo or Dublin, Paris or Panajachel. We'd seen the *Mona Lisa* and the *Last Supper*, visited Yellowstone and the Nile. We'd ridden elephants and danced the tango.

We were the translators, waitresses, cooks, English teachers, musicians, farm workers, writers. Some of us had married Egyptian engineers and been transferred to Italy. Some of us had fallen in love with Italian jazz musicians and been invited to live in villas beside medieval castles. Some of us had become neighbours, borrowing electrical converters instead of cups of sugar. Hanging out windows for chats in our own language.

It all sounded so glamorous, until you knew what we'd done to get there.

There were the tables we'd waited on, the potatoes we'd dug, the industrial texts on vacuum maintenance we'd translated. The boxes we'd packed and crammed into our parents' attics. The plants we'd given away. The hand-made pottery too fragile to ship. The baggage. Which blouse was the most wrinkle-prone? Which favourite sweater too heavy? There were the planes. The jetlag. The long waits in airport lounges and customs line-ups. The queries of border guards. The complications of living a life between the lines. Of visas and health-care and taxation. The bureaucracy of being a foreigner everywhere we went, even our own country.

"Where are you from?" a customer once asked as I'd served his pint of Keith's.

"Here," I'd answered, gesturing towards a grey Vancouver sky.

"But you have an accent," he insisted. "Irish, French?" I'm a hybrid, I might have said if I'd known it at the time. But how would he have understood?

Who but a fellow hybrid understood what it meant to speak the survival lingo of ten languages, to know the inner workings of a Mexican bus station? Who but a hybrid understood the art of riding a bus for eight hours without a pee break, wedged between a holy man smeared in ash and an overweight Sikh schoolteacher?

Who else understood the feeling of arriving, again and again, in a new place for the first time? The thrill. The loneliness. The stripped-bare feeling of a room empty of any pretext of you. Wondering who had existed before the potted plant was set on the sill and book placed by the bedside? Who understood venturing out into the New World and asking the baker for a loaf of bread? Pointing, shyly, towards the loaf topped with sesame seeds. No, not the one with a slash down the middle. No, not the one the baker placed in the bag. Who paid anyway simply because they knew no word of protest?

Not many understood that these things required sensitivity, strength, intelligence, finesse.

Still there were people who asked, "How was your trip?" – as if we'd done nothing but return evenly tanned from an all-inclusive resort. Hybrids did not take trips. We lived somewhere. We learned the language and ate the food. We took the bus, walked, hitchhiked if we had to. We worked if there was work and volunteered if there wasn't. We talked to our neighbours. We immersed ourselves in the tastes, smells, sights, and sounds of streets wandered and people met.

We answered the "How was your trip?" question every time, but rarely did anyone want to listen beyond the part about the weather, the food, the amusing anecdote – a near-kidnapping by a blue-robed Bedouin tribe, a Ladakhi bank manager who advised, "You must eat yak butter," before stamping a travellers cheque.

Eyes glazed over when we talked about the family in Guatemala living seven to a room in a tin-roofed shack. When we expounded upon the virtues of cultures different from our own. On the merits of European markets bursting with local produce and stores that closed from one to four p.m. On feeling safer in an Indian city of five million than in Toronto. On people who knew how to bathe with two cups of water. On mothers whose children were content to make kites from tissue paper and string.

This is when we realized that no matter how hard we tried, we would never fit in again. We could never be Katy from New Zealand or Angela from Canada. The lines had blurred too much; we'd shape-shifted one too many times. We were destined to wander desolately through the ethnic foods section at Safeway, to speak with accents that weren't our own.

We could never just go back home and hang out like we used to. Family and friends would notice, eventually, that something had changed. They'd guess that we'd tasted, smelled, seen, and heard too much. It could be a piece of unusual jewellry that gave us away, a tinkly laugh, an unusual answer to a straightforward question.

It could be that our eyes glazed over when others talked about Junior's first step, mortgage payments, curtain rods.

It could be that all those hours on planes, trains, buses, boats – all those invisible distances we'd travelled – revealed themselves somehow, like a comet's tail, resplendent, but too bright for the naked eye. People would become uncomfortable around us. We'd become the hippy, the bohemian. We'd become the eccentric, the thirty-something spinster. The crazy aunt. But no matter what they called us, we'd keep moving.

OUR EXPIRATION DATE

"Doesn't he know he'll miss out on sex and chocolate?" a friend asked.

"Is he gay?" my father asked.

It had become some kind of a joke, the decision Giuseppe had made to become a Buddhist monk. The fact that he was Italian didn't help matters, or that he was a talented jazz musician trained at famous music schools in Milan and Boston.

"And he's going to give all that up?" they asked.

Yes, he was. His mother's lasagna. *Tiramisù*. The sterling silver flute and the saxophone from 1940s New York. And me.

He was going to give it all up and go to a monastery in northeast Thailand infamous for its poisonous snakes and stifling monsoon heat. There he would shave his head and wear saffron-coloured robes. There he would wake at three a.m., eat one meal a day, and meditate.

In retrospect, I wished I had kept my mouth shut. In my haste to seek comforting words, I'd forgotten that family and friends sometimes weren't as open-minded and understanding as we perceived them to be. Walls adorned with images of Buddhist temples, floors strewn with meditation cushions, and bookshelves spilling the beliefs of major world religions didn't imply anyone would sympathize with your boyfriend's decision to become a monk. Such objects had become commodities, as secular as kitchen appliances.

But it was too late now. The cat was out of the bag. One friend with an *Om* symbol tattooed on the base of her spine had even stopped talking to me. I had a feeling she thought I'd lost my edge, that my brain had become addled by living with a practicing Buddhist. It was true I rarely swore now, and didn't guzzle red wine every Friday night. "Please don't get all spiritual and boring on me," she'd warned months ago.

These reactions alarmed me. I understood it wasn't every day an Italian jazz musician chose to become a Buddhist monk. I understood it was almost impossible not to give a little chuckle, to wonder at the incredulity of it all.

But now that the laughter had died down, now that his flight was booked and possessions were being sold off, people's reactions had changed: "Well, there must be something he's trying to escape," they said, or, "It's just not natural to give up sex."

Why such opposition? What did Giuseppe's decision have to do with them? Everything. He was checking out. He was checking out of this world of career, marriage, house, children. He was giving up everything my friends and family held dear. And he was giving it up voluntarily.

He had spent years reflecting upon the life combo we were offered in this society and had concluded that none of it, not even sex or chocolate, truly made him happy. He had decided to look elsewhere for happiness – inside his own mind. A task that was difficult to achieve while playing the sax in a smoky nightclub to earn a buck. But I'd learned not to say this out loud. I just smiled and nodded now.

I smiled and nodded rather than suggest that Giuseppe's decision reminded me that every situation was impermanent. There was nothing here to rely upon that wasn't in a constant state of change. I just had to watch nature at work to know this. Or sit down for a few minutes, close my eyes and watch my mind scamper all over the place. Nothing remained fixed and permanent; if it did, we'd be dead.

These laws of nature weren't so easy to accept. Even though there was the usual talk of eternity in the first days of our meeting, and of marriage, all of this talk had slipped away into something we called the past. Our relationship had an expiration date now.

I confess none of this had been easy to accept. I'd had six months of denial that Giuseppe didn't really want to become a monk, that he wanted to drink cappuccino in the *piazza* with me and pretend it was enough. It took a three-day retreat at a Buddhist monastery on the outskirts of Rome to show me just how wrong I'd been. While there, I'd been annoyed by the resident monks, looking so content as they tended their herb gardens and ate my badly cooked pasta as though it were the most delicious thing they'd ever tasted. I'd kept my eyes open during the meditation sessions, watching Giuseppe as he sat so straight, his hands folded like a lotus. He'd looked at me at the train station in Rome and I knew what he was going to say. So I said it for him: "You still want to become a monk." He nodded.

There was only the present left now. And the present wasn't always a nice place to be. Anything could happen here, and it frightened us until we got used to it. No one wanted to admit that anything could take their loved ones away at any moment: a car accident, another woman, monkhood. The seemingly predictable life combo – career, marriage, house, children – was as unpredictable as the weather.

What was so wrong about seeking a stable core? Something so commonplace that it was said to exist inside each one of us, call it God, Buddha, or peace of mind.

What was so wrong about searching for it alone in a far-off jungle? Living simply in a hut, trying to do the least amount of harm in a world overrun by harming?

There was only the present now. To try to love without future expectations or clinging to the past. To try to understand that learning about the contents of your mind was as valid a pursuit as learning how to play a tricky riff.

It wasn't such a bad place, this present moment. I was learning a lot. In fact, even after Giuseppe's flight took off from Milan, I thought I might just stay there.

ROMA OSTIENSE TO ALESSANDRIA

THERE IS NO ROOM TO SIT and so we stand, pressed to the wall. We watch a family from Naples, closed in their glass compartment, eat crusty buns and *prosciutto*, drink red wine from white plastic cups. There was a time when I would have felt like screaming, like throwing something, or slamming a door. What else is there to do when your heart is yanked from your chest? But this is no place for all of that. This is a train. Every few minutes someone wants to get by to use the toilet, or buy an espresso, and I must press myself against the glass and face the dark pits of my eyes. I look like Death. And things are different now. You, for one thing, are different. You offer me pizza, or "Maybe some fruit juice?" You poke my shoulder when we're passing the sea. The Mediterranean. You know how much I like the sea. And I realize, finally, that this might be love. This moment that I turn and feel your shoulder shift to let me rest in its clutch. This moment when we know that everything will end, but it will end softened by the wool of your sweater and the blue of the water pulsing from track to track, until the next station. Until I collect my bags, button my coat, and disembark.

LONELINESS AND LONGING FOR RISOTTO

IN AISLE THREE OF DELMA'S CO-OP, I began to cry. But I kept pushing my cart past the creamed corn and bags of dusty-looking lentils. By the time I'd reached the snack foods, I'd calmed myself. It was only natural to feel overwhelmed in a grocery store with a soundtrack playing the chirping of songbirds. It was only natural to feel this way on an island an eight-hour ferry ride away from Prince Rupert, B.C. – the closest outpost with a movie theatre – on Canada's Northwest coast.

I decided to treat myself to some comfort food – a bag of lime-and-black-pepper potato chips that cost almost four dollars. I reminded myself that things were more expensive in the North. They'd travelled long distances by sea and air to arrive there, and then 110 kilometres on a road riddled with clear-cuts, bolting deer, and the occasional herd of wild cattle. I was lucky I didn't have to hunt and forage to survive up here. Really, no one had any business expecting to find a bag of carnaroli rice in the ethnic foods section. I should have been happy with a taco kit and a bottle of China Lily soy sauce.

Yes, just a few days ago I'd been living in Italy. But there was no need to talk about the delights of Italian markets, warm temperatures, and a boyfriend who did things like fold my fresh-off-the-line panties into perfect, origami-like squares. His charming accent was irrelevant now.

Now it was time to choose produce. The rumbling of a thunderstorm played as a fine mist settled over the wilted lettuce. I took a deep breath and moved along to things with longer shelf lives: apples, potatoes, squash. My mother had once told me it was important to eat well no matter how broken-hearted I felt. I loaded my cart with anything that hadn't begun to rot, disregarding the prices and the fact that it was almost summer and I was buying items fit for a Thanksgiving feast.

While living in Guatemala, David had told me he thought it crazy anyone should choose to live in the North. He'd visited Montréal in January, and that was enough to convince him all Canadians were nuts. "I never once left the underground malls," he'd drawled while swinging on his hammock. "I feared for my life."

I'd argued we had four seasons – including summers hot enough for air-conditioning. But that was before I'd lived on Canada's Northwest coast.

I zipped up my puffy black MEC vest and loaded my groceries. On the drive along Tow Hill Road, the trees were just starting to unfurl their leaves. The first time I'd travelled this road, one of those "this is it" feelings had welled up inside me. The sky had been very blue. The trees as multifaceted as emeralds flashing in the sunlight. At a bend in the road, a sherry-coloured river mouth, grassy dunes, and a great swath of topaz ocean had burst into view. That feeling had kept me here months longer than I'd intended to stay. On a second visit, only an offer to live in Italy had pulled me away.

But now I was wondering why I'd returned. There was nothing here, just the odd house with smoke snaking from its chimney into a grey sky. I stopped just before the sign for Naikoon Provincial Park, at my last chance to make contact – a phone booth. I called Italy. No answer. I left a message in a tiny voice. "Help!" I felt like crying.

Maybe David had been right to choose to live in a country where you could sleep naked and walk barefoot and flowers bloomed year-round.

I turned off the ignition. For the first time in several days, I stopped moving. I stood still beneath the gigantic spruce guarding the cabin's front door. I breathed. I'd forgotten how fresh air could be. I breathed in air that had been filtered by oceans of evergreens and laced with saltwater mists.

For the first time in a long while, I was alone. Not the kind of alone when I'd been sipping cappuccino in the *piazza*. No one was going to walk up this dirt path through the forest.

Not many people, besides another Canadian, would understand the sense of possibility that arose on truly reaching the North. It was a feeling of liberty of the rarest kind. Perhaps it was reward for braving the elements and eating wilted produce. It was cold and nothing would bloom for awhile. But I was alone and the air was fresh. I could squat on the moss and pee if I wanted to. Sing at the top of my lungs.

It began to rain. A heavy-looking axe leaned against the woodshed. It was time to pick up that axe and split logs down their seams. There was no such thing as gentleness here. I had to learn quickly to be tough – it was the only way to keep warm. I picked up the axe. This was it. I swung, hoping to hit the right spot.

DEAR JESSICA

NOT MUCH HAS CHANGED since that morning when the sunrise barely made its mark in the sky because the smog was so thick. You and I were on the rooftop doing downward-facing dogs. I started crying for some reason or another. You kept your arms straight, heels pushed to the ground, and listened. We went for a walk through alleyways filled with vendors selling bangles, nose-rings, and *bindis*. Later we painted our toenails, blood red, up there on that rooftop, just as the sun was setting and the kites rose into the sky. Now I'm crying again. A different place. A different posture. I feel like that sunrise that couldn't make its mark in the sky. I know this will pass. I just have to think of those kites, the ones that broke free from their strings, how they soared for a few moments, startled by such freedom. How they fell so gracefully then, into the boughs of *bodhi* trees.

THE SOUNDS OF SILENCE

THEY SAY SILENCE IS GOLDEN. I've searched for it far and wide, not even knowing what I was looking for, at first. The quest began in the spring of 1999 on Inis Mór, an island off the west coast of Ireland. I was twenty-eight at the time. My days were spent digging potato drills. Dermot, the farmer who'd been foolish enough to take me on as a volunteer WWOOFer (World Wide Opportunities on Organic Farms) said, "I've never met a woman who can handle a shovel like you."

Dermot would never guess that my shovel fervour was rage-induced. Every thrust was a blow to the red-headed woman with whom Michel had fallen in love. As I dug I imagined her standing by the pine kitchen table I'd sanded by hand, mincing onions with the Henckel knife I'd forgotten when I'd driven away with all the possessions I could fit into our Subaru. I hated them both and the potatoes knew it. Dermot should have been afraid. Instead, he told the islanders, a tight-knit clan of Gaelic speakers whose ancestors had survived the Great Famine of 1845-1849 and were wary of all blow-ins (anyone who hadn't lived there since 500 AD), that I was a brilliant worker. Work offers poured in. Soon I was cleaning toilets at Mainistir House Hostel, waitressing at The Bayview, and planting arugula at The Man of Aran Cottages. I rode a bike to all those places, usually against a wind that could blow you to a standstill and whisked the North Atlantic into a froth that crashed against 350-foot-high cliffs until the ground shook.

I was so busy cycling, scrubbing, brewing tea, and digging that I scarcely noticed I'd come to one of the most peaceful places on earth, a place people fantasized about, planning week-long visits years in advance. I met some of those people at the Man of Aran Cottages while tending the roses – clipping and tying with savage precision – as I imagined Michel and his new love listening to Jacques Brel, to our song, "Ne Me Quitte Pas," the lyrics playing over and over in my head.

I met the silent seekers as they sat gazing out at a sparkly sea with the mountains of Connemara as a backdrop. They had a look in their eye, like they'd been drugged. They sat on picnic tables beside whitewashed cottages, novels face-down, staring straight ahead. It was Paulette from Paris who spoke to me first. "You must feel so at peace living here," she said. I dead-headed the roses, imagining someone else's fiery little head resting in my palm. I tossed the petals to the wind and smiled. Paulette told me how she'd dreamed of coming here for years, but she'd been too busy, first with family, then with her career as a curator for the Louvre. And now she could finally just sit for hours on end, drinking the silence like a fine French wine. "This is one of the last silent places in Europe."

Silence. Is that what I'd heard the day I'd arrived, while waiting for Dermot in Kilronan? The tide had been out. There were no cars. No wind. Just a sound as though the air had been sucked up into the wide swath of sky and stretched taut against the grey. Just air scrubbed clean by wind and rain, empty of anything but the present. I'd panicked, examining the present moment for the first time. Stone buildings. Stone walls. A stone-coloured sea. Nothing but cold, dead, silent stone. What on earth was I doing here? I'd watched the ferry head back to bustling, crayon-box-of-colours, flowers-in-the-window-box Galway City. The last ferry. I was stuck. Stuck with twenty pounds to my name and a broken heart.

Obviously Paulette thought I was one of them. One of the silent ones. She didn't realize I did everything I could to fill my hours with as much sound as possible. Sound was my friend. Sound was life. If it wasn't the battery-operated radio, it was the guitarist roommate from County Cavan who knew every Irish folk song by heart. It was the Walkman. It was the cello-playing, ballad-singing Nickie. It was the football match at Tí Joe Macs, the Irish dancing at Tigh Fitz, the cover band at Joe Watty's.

Silence scared me. Especially on those days I hiked along the cliffs, singing "The Dawning of the Day" until I arrived at Dún Dúchathair, the Black Fort. Here, enclosed by ringfort walls, the Atlantic was finally muffled. The wind stilled. There was a feeling that I should whisper, tread lightly, that maybe the rocks had eyes. It was an eerie kind of place, but I was drawn there more and more as spring turned to summer, as the potatoes sprouted, and wildflowers burst forth from the grikes.

The Black Fort became a place of refuge from my non-stop noisy thoughts – Michel and his *petit chou* now in the throes of a Montréal summer, likely sunbathing at Parc Lafontaine, drinking *La Fin du Monde* at outdoor terraces. I lay on the sun-warmed stone, drinking my first taste of silence. Paulette had been right – this stuff was good, addictive, even. I lay on the stone staring up at the sky until my ears pricked up – tourists. Clatter of shale. Voices amplified across fields of limestone. The Italian tour groups. The lads from Dublin. I was annoyed before I even saw their faces. Annoyed by their feckless joy at making noise. I skittered along the cliffs like a wild animal being pursued until it was safe again, until it was silent.

In the eleven years since I first went to Ireland, I'd climbed Chichén Itzá, rowed down the Ganges, lived beside a Renaissance-era castle in Italy. I'd moved to an off-the-grid cabin called the Spare Girl in the middle of a temperate rainforest on Canada's Northwest coast.

It was there, on Haida Gwaii, that I read *One Square Inch of Silence: One Man's Quest to Preserve Quiet,* in which acoustic ecologist Gordon Hempton asks: "Have you heard the rain lately?" That summer of 2010, I definitely heard the rain. It fell hour after hour, day after day. The pattering upon cedar plank roof, the drip-drip-drip, the streaming from eavestrough to water barrel, the gush of a thousand pregnant black clouds whose water had broken – I knew the sound well.

Gordon Hempton travelled the world to prove what I feared: silence is an endangered species. Fewer and fewer places exist on this planet where you can sit for twenty minutes without hearing the noise of human activity. Thrum of traffic, hum of refrigerator, rumble of jetliner. But noise-cancelling headphones and triple-glazed windows aren't the solution. "Silence is not the absence of something but the presence of everything," Hempton says. Silence can only be found in the natural soundscape – the sound of the rain, the "falling whisper of the snow," the "passing flock of chestnut-backed chickadees." Hempton set out across America in a 1964 VW bus to record a sonic EKG of the country, measuring the dropping of a maple leaf (thirty decibels), the distant call of an owl (thirty-five decibels), the hum of insect wings (twenty-four decibels), a starry night on the prairie (eighteen decibels). Within these natural EKGs we can find our birthright, the sounds our ears have been perfectly evolved to hear. We can find ourselves.

I wanted to find myself. But how could I when my Haida Gwaii neighbours fired up their chainsaws while I was listening to the chestnut-backed chickadees swoop from spruce bough to spruce bough? When the Albertans rode through the sand dunes in their ATVs? When the clam diggers roared down Tow Hill Road in their pick-up trucks? I wanted to find myself. I wanted to see what lay buried beneath the din of thirty-nine years of chatter.

I took the batteries out of the clock. I listened to the rain. I listened for weeks. And then the winds began. Hurricane-force winds that started as an innocent rustling of alder leaves and progressed to a banshee-filled freight train whomping the cabin, sending the woodsmoke running down the stove pipe and into the kitchen. I listened to the silence until I couldn't bear it for another second.

I drove in search of insulated walls rather than driftwood logs chinked by moss and newspaper. I was beginning to understand, finally, in a deep, experiential sense of the word, that nature wasn't a docile thing filled with birdsong and a spring breeze blowing through the trees. Nature was no more static than silence was empty. Nature was full, full of the sound and the fury. And I was nature.

And so I found myself. Drinking a vanilla latté at The Ground on Haida Gwaii. I tried to do what I'd learned in India – breathe. *Inhale-One-Exhale-Two.* I tried to listen to the natural soundscape of my mind. Instead I heard myself thinking about the ridiculous price of the bag of cherries I'd just bought, the way Surfer Jeff had looked at me at the post office (did he like me or was he just stoned?), the rumour of an earthquake, the program on CBC about biophilia, the student loan repayment assistance plan application form.

Even back at the Spare Girl, where it was quiet enough to hear a huckleberry drop on the moss, the inner noise persisted. Should I order wood from Smokin' Joe or Kevin Deacock? Should I make focaccia for the potluck?

Would I ever hear the silence of the natural soundscape with a mind like the one Goenka described during those evenings at Dhamma Bodhi in India? A mind "so wild, like a wild animal, a monkey mind, grasping one branch after another." It all sounded so good, this search for silence. *Inhale-One-Exhale-One.* Surf crashing. *Inhale-Two-Exhale-Two.* Branch cracking.

NABOB TINS AND TURKISH CARPETS

WE STOOD AT GATE C AND my mother began to cry. She'd been saying good-bye to me for twenty years, since I'd first left home and flew to Frankfurt from Toronto. There had been ferry terminal, bus station, front porch, campground, car-door, and at least a dozen more airport good-byes. She cried no matter where we were and regardless of whether it would be a month or a year till we met again. Once she told me that watching your child leave home, even if she was a fully-grown woman, was "like ripping your heart out and watching it walk through the door."

Every time I left it became clearer and clearer that I, her only daughter, would never settle down. We'd never sew curtains together or examine carpet swatches. We'd never re-paint the bathroom. This wouldn't have been all that important if my mother wasn't a domestic goddess – the type of person who knew how to remove any type of stain, who ironed her sheets. Of course she'd be driven to tears by a daughter who'd never owned an iron, who'd always slept on futons, and stored her clothing in milk crates.

It hadn't always been like this. There were times when I'd dreamed of three-bedroom houses and picket fences. When my mother and I had shopped happily for clothes together – feminine garb – things that called for ironing and matching tights. There had been talk of marrying at twenty-one and bearing three children. This must have been when my mother had started to save things for me – silverware, china, linens. She never envisioned they'd be stored in her mahogany armoire forever.

Those had been the late-teens, early-twenties years when my mother still had hope, when she called her daughter "my little gypsy." When she'd thought it was all a phase.

There was no hope now. Now, I felt like crying with her. I was about to return to my remote refuge on Canada's west coast – The Spare Girl cabin. It was built from items salvaged on the beach, and looked it. Nothing was finished. The logs were rough: chinked with moss and newspaper and a decades worth of dust, cat fur, ash, and who knew what else. Nails stuck out of the ceiling. Window frames were mismatched, their paint peeling. Carpenter ants nested in a perpetually damp corner where the eavestrough dripped into the rain buckets. Occasionally, piles of fine sawdust drifted down to let you know they were busy at the work of chewing the house down.

You didn't have to be a person who grew up in a six-bedroom Victorian farmhouse with all the luxuries of the day to be puzzled by your daughter's most recent choice of abode. Sometimes I wondered about it myself. Sometimes I thought it might be nice to wake up in the morning and simply settle onto a warm toilet seat and go about my business rather than don a pair of rubber boots and trudge uphill through salal and huckleberry bushes to reach an outhouse. Sometimes it might be nice to turn on a tap and feel warm water cascade down my shoulders rather than fill a five-litre pot with rainwater, heat it on the woodstove, then funnel it into a bag fitted with a nozzle the size of a quarter.

But such inconveniences had their charms. There was something to be said about doing your business beneath a stand of towering spruce, or standing naked outdoors while showering to the sound of a thrush. There was something to be said for the cabin itself, how it felt like living inside a tree. It felt alive. An array of giant windows on all sides deepened this feeling. There were no escaping glimpses of ocean, sky, forest. Sound permeated the walls – raindrops, wind, birdsong, surf. I felt part of something much bigger than myself.

But I feared my mother wouldn't appreciate these charms when she came to visit. I couldn't really expect her to be a good sport about the black plastic stapled to the north side of the cabin, or the free-range chickens forever unearthing mysterious-looking fragments of garbage. It would be clearer than ever that Grandma's silver tea-service would never be displayed on the cedar plank propped up by two giant Nabob tins that served as a side table.

A less stubborn daughter would have given in years ago. She would have settled into the type of place where you could lay down the Turkish carpet and prop up the antique china cabinet in the corner. She would have sat with her mother at the oak dining-room table carved with wreaths of flowers and poked napkins through ivory holders and discussed things like baby showers and Christmas cake recipes and family reunion picnics. They would have gotten to know one another amongst the solidity and endurance of such objects. They could have forged a bond on the rims of their porcelain tea cups, sipping where generations had sipped before.

Instead my mother had been forced to find other ways to bond with me. She'd visited me in a dirt-floored adobe hut in Guatemala, a renovated pig shed in Ireland. She'd endured gastrointestinal disorders, gale-force winds, scurrying rats. Nothing had been as straightforward and comfortable as she may have wished. And I had to admit I admired her. I admired her because she cried at Gate C but not once had she asked me not to board the plane.

When she came to visit, she would bear gifts suited to her daughter's nomadic lifestyle – colourful dishcloths, paper napkins printed with poppies. She would sit down by the woodstove pretending not to notice the soot-stained wall. She would suggest sewing curtains for the kitchen window – something bright and simple – and this time, instead of telling her not to bother, I thought I'd offer to help.

BARING ALL TO RESIDENT SQUIRREL

TODAY IS SHOWER DAY. No small feat during a water shortage. The water comes all the way from the municipal tap in Masset, sixteen and a half kilometres down Tow Hill Road. I've been hauling it home in a variety of plastic containers, as our rain barrels have been dry for weeks.

AN OFF-THE-GRID SHOWER:

1. Heat hauled hauled water on wood-stove until perfect temperature
2. Pour water into coffee pot, funnel into Stearns Sun Shower (a heavy-duty plastic bag with a nine-litre capacity)
3. Stand on chair and hang shower bag on nail jutting out from cedar log on south side of cabin
4. Retrieve towel and undress
5. Walk outdoors to bare all to Sitka spruce, salal, huckleberry, and the resident squirrel
6. Unscrew nozzle. Feel wind on wet skin. Watch a canopy of leaves shimmer in the sunlight
7. If necessary to wash hair twice (and it's always necessary), ensure to save enough water to rinse out conditioner
8. Stoke fire in woodstove. Stand in front while drying off. Enjoy smelling clean for ten minutes – the amount of time it takes to smell like woodsmoke again

ST. MARY'S SPRING

"BE CAREFUL OF THE WATER,," my friend said and patted her belly with that special smile reserved for expectant mothers.

I'd seen that smile before. By now, almost all my friends had smiled that smile at least once. The smile said: I am woman. Fertile. You could do this too. ·

But I was careful of the water. Very careful. Especially now that I was living off the grid where my only source of water fell from the sky. Who knows what happened to it up there.

I collected rainwater in garbage pails that sat beneath an eavestrough. When it rained, which was often, a steady stream filtered through pieces of window screen stretched taut across the pails. The screens were meant to inhibit mosquitoes – and other creatures of Naikoon forest – from breeding. But they weren't always stretched taut enough.

When the pails were full, water ran from a rubber hose snaked through a hole in the wall of the log cabin to a faucet at the sink. It tasted slightly of bark and cedar needle. I was careful with it. I boiled it every time, a full, roiling boil.

It wasn't only the rainwater to be wary of around here. Not far from my doorstep lay Dixon Entrance – entranceway to a Pacific Ocean swimming with Haida creation myths. It was here, just a few kilometres up the coastline, where Raven was said to have discovered a gigantic clamshell filled with the first humans. Here, where he coaxed them out upon the sands, where they bred and had children that are said to have been strong and fierce, children of a wild west coast. Children of the water.

In the opposite direction lay St. Mary's spring. Legend has it if you drink from the spring you will return to the islands in the future. Twice I'd drunk, and twice I'd returned from places where I was perfectly happy – a hilltop room with a view of the valley of Kathmandu, and a villa beside a medieval castle in Italy.

So you can see why I was wary of these waters. It was too easy while living in a place like this to get caught up in the mystery and power of nature. A place where people's ties to sea and land were still intimate.

Where they dug razor clams and dried chanterelles. Where they knew tide tables better than TV guides.

It seemed only natural here to follow nature's call, to down rainwater with relish, to do what nature did best – procreate.

And there was nothing like nature to get you in the mood. A surf pounded rhythmically. A sky swelled with lush clouds. Evergreens exuded dark, heady scent. Air was laced with a northern chill, even in the height of summer, forcing you to light a crackling fire and seek out a warm body to share your bed. As the days shortened, the danger grew. I'd been told that islanders began their search for a winter mate after Labour Day, or else held on tight to the ones they already had. It was during these months to take heed, I'd been warned. It was during these months to be careful of the water.

That was why I'd been thinking of switching to bottled. Ferrying in litres of the stuff – treated and sterile. Void of life.

I knew that having a child was probably the closest I could come to producing a miracle. I just didn't want one. It wasn't because my biological clock wasn't ticking or I hadn't found the "right man." It wasn't because I didn't like children – I had three nieces and a nephew I'd loved since the moment they were born. I'd witnessed friends' babies grow into walking, talking beings capable of great acts of kindness. I had no doubt children were miraculous. But I thought there were enough of them now.

Experts said our planet was bursting at its seams. My time in India had been enough for me to believe them. There I'd witnessed villagers crowd around a pail of water to wash themselves, and children fight with feral dogs over mouldy *chapatis*.

It was difficult to imagine an overcrowded world while sitting on an isolated beach watching the tide come in. In two hours, two people would pass. What harm could one more tiny being do? Especially a cute one with blonde ringlets who liked to build sandcastles and walk along the shore holding my hand? But I still didn't want to smile that smile.

It wasn't an easy choice to make. It wasn't something celebrated with balloons and cigars. Maybe because it seemed to go against the flow of nature. But nature was changing: ice caps were melting, resources dwindling.

What did all this mean for a woman living on Canada's Northwest coast, for those children in India? How long before we'd all be fighting for those mouldy *chapatis*?

THE MOON OVER NAIKOON

FORGET ABOUT BOOK TOURS or reading engagements. Forget about "branding" yourself and promoting your work to the unseen masses. Just get a job at the Moon Over Naikoon and bring along a pile of books. Here you will meet a photographer from New York City, a cellist from Scotland, a local fisherman. And all of them will buy your poetry book. While the coffee percolates, they will ask what your book is about and you will tell them stories about hitchhiking to Mexico with a French Canadian you met while tree planting, about your thatched cottage on a rocky isle in Ireland. You will talk until interrupted by the next in line asking about the daily soup, or "What kind of muffins are those?"

You will cream butter and sugar, and then you will listen. You'll hear about serving in Vietnam, about guarding a Buddhist monastery carved into stone, a spiral staircase descending into the centre of the Earth. "The monks would go down there for weeks to meditate," they'll tell you. The family from Washington State building a house down the road will tell you about travelling on business to India, Bangladesh, China, about countrysides filled with factories, and entire towns unable to breathe.

The dough will finish its first rising, and when you punch it down for its second, the man who works for the Ministry of Agriculture will peruse the "read local" books for sale and notice Susan Musgrave's name. "She lives down the road," you'll say.

"I love this cover," he'll say of a deer lying dead in the snow, of the title *When the World is Not Our Home.*

"So do I," you'll agree. And you'll look at one another then, understanding something. And he'll buy your book, too.

After this sale you'll realize you're doing what you've always wanted to do. For a few moments, you're entering the life of another. More importantly, they're allowing you to do so – they're even paying you for it. You'll stand there greasing loaf pans while they read about the little boy tortured in Guatemala, your friend dying of cancer, your heart breaking again and again. After a few minutes, they'll look at you differently. They'll thank you.

And you will want to thank them for much more than their twenty bucks. You'll want to thank them for making poetry, for what else could this exchange be called? This chance encounter transformed into a moment of shared humanity? You'll want to thank them for making you realize it's possible to feel a little more at home in this world. But they'll leave before you can tell them all this. They'll see you're busy, that there are people waiting in line.

WHERE THE PACIFIC MEETS THE SANGAN

TODAY, A FAMOUS POET WALKS into the Moon over Naikoon and orders a grilled cheese. She talks about her preference for shortbread over scones, rainwater over tap water, of how she sleeps in an opium bed once slept in by David Bowie and Mick Jagger, and the time she lived in London back in '75. "I don't know who's writing there these days," she says, biting into her grilled cheese. She sits at the table beside the sea lion skulls and the shell fossils, her eyes flicking from the huckleberry muffins to the spinal disc of a humpback. The talk turns to wind turbines and peat bogs, and her finger taps the small hollow of her throat, searching for the right word to describe where the Pacific meets the Sangan. Her eyes flick from coffee urn to moon snail to the yellow cedar floor, and you could almost hear the tap...tap... tap... of a finger searching for the right word to describe how the May light gathers in pools across its surface.

THE SPARE GIRL

"GRAB A SLEEPING BAG AND go to Colin's place," Meredith said above the cell-phone static. "You're blocked in. Trees are down. This wind is strange, and it's making me nervous."

I hung up the phone and another gust rocked the little cedar-log cabin. Thunder rumbled. Lightning struck. Rain pelted the cedar-plank roof without mercy.

Another gust hit. The wind turbine made the noise it made when wind speeds were higher than usual. Imagine a giant bed sheet made of metal hung on a clothes line snapping in the wind. That night it sounded like the bed sheet was as big as the sky.

Was I safe here? The answer came quickly: Yes. I'd weathered many a storm in the Spare Girl cabin. I'd arrived almost three years ago with a broken heart, and the Spare Girl had been my refuge ever since. I'd learned how to split wood and tend a fire. I'd learned that every drop of water I consumed to bathe, cook, and clean fell from the sky. I'd been too busy surviving to remember things like feeling sad. But when I remembered, when I sat by the fire and watched my whole life go up in flames, the eighty cedar logs stood firm. I knew I was safe in their embrace.

I'd spent a lot of time alone in this cabin. Many times I'd cried myself to sleep – especially on dark winter nights when the wood was damp and I couldn't get a fire going. I'd spent weeks listening to wind – southeasters, northwesters, all directions between – blowing through the chinks. I'd watched hundred-foot trees bend like blades of grass. Coldness, darkness, the relentless cry of the wind – these were the things that had tried my spirit. With no central heating, stable power source, or insulation, I was forced to confront the reality of the elements, and how alone they could make me feel. Again and again, I'd been humbled into realizing that I was a creature of the elements. I was a creature of light, warmth. And company.

I'd hosted dinner parties in this cabin with the types of friends one could only hope to meet at the end of the road at the tip of an island archipelago. I'd read countless books – of opera singers in Central America, novelists living on Capri. I'd watched a tortoise-shell cat sleeping on the bed in a pool of sunlight.

And I'd touched the logs of the cabin walls, every single day, wondering what life still coursed through them. There was reason to believe their embrace wasn't just imagined, that no matter how alone I may have felt, it was impossible to be alone. Even during a hurricane, I was safe.

THIS THING CALLED COMMUNITY

I HAVE A P.O. BOX AND a bank account at the local branch. The cashiers at Delma's Co-op know my name. I own waxed paper, three sets of sheets, a hot water bottle. I arrived here with a backpack, and now my possessions would easily fill my Toyota Corolla. But it's more than that: I have friends. Friends I've grown to love and depend upon. And I have this thing called a community – people who will change a flat tire for me, or come to hear me read poetry, even if they don't like poetry.

For years, while travelling alone in the kinds of places I've never told my mother about, my life often depended upon the kindness of strangers. Now it depends upon this community. I think of all the things that could go wrong while living off-grid sixteen and a half kilometres from town, and who I could call for help. The list is long. In fact, I know I could call anyone with a phone number and they would come to my aid. This comforts me. Who do I thank for the gift of such a comfort on such a remote and windswept archipelago?

And who do I thank for the continuum of gestures that make a gypsy feel at home? Thank you for the gift of blackcurrant jelly, for the loan of your truck. Thank you for stacking my firewood and picking up my library books. Thank you for saying you wish I could stay whenever I think it's time to go.

Last night, an older and wiser friend said it's these types of gestures that create community. Not potlucks and loonie auctions and clothing swaps. It's not about being somewhere you think you should be. It's about doing something. Something that may seem insignificant. As she turned to cream the butter and sugar, I realized, as usual, that she was right.

Today I wonder if community could mean a place of common humanity rather than common residence, if we need a place to call home to create it. As the north wind continues to blow and the water barrels freeze, I wonder if community could fit into my backpack. For when I leave, as all gypsies must, I hope you'll travel with me this time. You, the one who left a bottle of salal wine on my kitchen table, who changed my oil free of charge, who always remembers my name.

WOMAN IN BLUE BATHROBE

THE DAY BEGAN WITH A CAT sitting on my chest. Then a blue fleece bathrobe and slippers. I walked down the stairs to the semi-darkness of the kitchen. I could see my breath. Penelope ate her teaspoon of Fancy Feast. I pulled on my rubber boots and walked up the path to the outhouse. I almost slipped on the ice. By now, Dark Star, my absent neighbour's black Lab, had arrived. Hungry. She watched me pee.

Still in blue bathrobe, we walked to her food bowl. Then I walked to the chicken coop and unlatched the door. First the ducks ran out, beating their wings, and then the chickens flew down from their roosts. I broke the ice on their bathtub full of rainwater with the heel of my boot.

Still in blue bathrobe, I split kindling. I crumpled up balls of newspaper and prayed the fire would start. I turned the oven to Broil to take the chill off. I turned on the faucet. No water. Still in blue bathrobe, I put on my rubber boots. I walked to the water barrel that didn't seem to freeze as quickly as the others. I plunged a bucket into water floating with ice shards.

Still in blue bathrobe, I watched the fire spark and crackle and then peter out. For the past week I'd been struggling to ignite the roaring flames essential to my warmth. Several people had told me their theories about my fire-starting dysfunction – maybe I wasn't grounded enough. Maybe the fire sensed my impatience. Maybe the fire knew I was leaving soon.

Yesterday, a Haida Elder with whom I'd worked for nearly three years at the transition house in Masset – a safe place for women and children who had experienced violence – had visited while I'd struggled. She'd looked at the smouldering fire, then at me, and I awaited her words of wisdom. "That thing needs to be cleaned out," Margaret said. For the first time all week, I noticed the embarrassing layer of debris and ash that had accumulated after numerous attempts to fuel the fire with anything remotely combustible. I closed the woodstove door. Margaret laughed.

Yes, I was leaving. Soon. The Haida had been to bid me farewell. The daily chores had acquired a new poignancy. I did them in silence. I'd begun to see myself as a character in a documentary. I imagined a camera panning from hatchet to red bucket to spruce crowns. I wondered if I could appear in my blue bathrobe in every scene. I did my chores, slowly, so the camera could get a good shot. It was important this was well documented. Watch as I sit in the chair by the fire and drink Earl Grey. Watch as I walk down the path towards the Pacific. The sky is streaked with winter rose. Dark Star chases after the sandpipers. Can you see Alaska in the distance, fresh snow on the chain of peaks? Can you see the woman in a blue bathrobe, head bowed against the wind?

epilogue

THE SLOW LANE

WHEN I DISEMBARK THE Inside Passage ferry in Port Hardy, B.C., I quickly learn to pay attention. I am befuddled by noonday sun and blinking lights, by lane merges and left-turn arrows. My Toyota Corolla is packed with all my possessions and Penelope. She sits in her carrier case beside a box filled with bottles of elderflower wine. I look in the rearview mirror, trying to see above the totes crammed with clothing and books and items I couldn't bear to leave behind – an antique oil lamp, a yew cutting board, two porcelain tea cups.

For weeks my neighbours asked me why I was leaving. I told them it was to find work, to pay off debts, to be closer to family. None of those answers satisfied them. "But this is your home," they insisted.

As I get my bearings, other vehicles begin to pass. Those stuck behind me rev with impatience. No one knows that the last road the wheels of my car touched was a Haida Gwaii road. A road without stoplights or collector lanes.

Soon Campbell River is upon me and I hold firm to the steering wheel, navigating my way through the streets like I'm crossing a war zone. Then it's Nanaimo. Then the horror of the Trans-Canada Highway.

You would think I've never driven before. But I've been driving for nearly twenty-four years. By eighteen, I had driven from the Black Forest to Berlin on German *autobahns* and throughout the Swiss Alps. While living in Montréal, I cruised the streets in a 1970s cargo van. In Arizona I navigated the White Mountains in a Ford pickup. I've driven east and west on Southern Ontario's Highway 401 more times than I can count. I've driven from Vancouver to Toronto multiple times.

I used to hop in the car and drive ten hours to see an ocean or a desert cactus. I used to love to drive. But Haida Gwaii changed all that.

Now I dread sitting behind the wheel while vehicles barrel past me on all sides. They move so fast my car shakes. I dread the neon headlights of a monster pickup truck burning into my rearview mirror from behind. I dread the sound of a fully loaded logging truck trying to gear down. I dread seeing the wooden crosses and fresh flowers adorning trees and utility poles. No one slows down to pay their respects. They are all in too much of a hurry.

But what I dread most is becoming like everyone else. Already, my speedometer has risen from eighty kilometres an hour to ninety. To one hundred. The farmer's field, the view of the mountains, the sign for a winery – all these things have become more and more meaningless. Less and less part of some grander journey. As I accelerate, I become just another person trying to get somewhere and get there as quickly as possible.

Haida Gwaii taught me that getting somewhere quickly was a futile pursuit. Mostly because there weren't many places to go. There was one main road. People drove fast on that road, but not without taking time to wave. They waved almost apologetically as they pulled up alongside you to take the lead. They waved as they approached in the oncoming lane. And at certain times of year, the deer population caused nearly everyone to slow down. Even hardened drivers of big trucks didn't want to hit fawns and their doting mothers.

Perhaps when you drive up and down the same road all the time and you see the same sights, you realize that it's never the same road or the same view. It's always different. The sea, the sky, the trees. Everything is always changing, if you slow down enough to notice. There's no need to rush from A to B because you realize your life actually exists between those two letters.

No one on the Trans-Canada Highway will let me live between the letters. As I drive, I fear for my life. I listen to soothing cello suites and piano sonatas. I adorn the Corolla with hanging crystals and Hindu gods for protection. I breathe deeply, pretending I'm driving down Tow Hill Road on my favourite stretch, the unpaved part, where the cedar boughs drape over the road, creating a tunnel of green.

But it's difficult to ignore the strip malls and parking lots, the headlights boring into me like the eyes of a creature possessed. It's difficult not to drive faster, to get out of this hell, quick. I accelerate past one hundred kilometres an hour without realizing my speed. It's a heady feeling. For a few moments, I cruise alongside everyone else. No one seems to notice. There are no waves of camaraderie.

Then I slow down, mostly because I'm going uphill. I see the mountains tinged with snow. I see a river below. Wherever this life is taking me, I want to get there below the speed limit.

NOTES

THE EVENTS IN THIS BOOK took place between 1992 and 2010. During this time I travelled to more than a dozen countries and met hundreds of people. But only a fraction of these experiences are included in *Every Day We Disappear*. Within this narrative, two journeys to India (2006 and 2009) and two occasions when I lived on Haida Gwaii (2007, and 2008 to 2011) are merged for the sake of storytelling. Please forgive any gaps in time or space. Information gleaned from three *Lonely Planet: India* guidebooks, published by Lonely Planet Global Limited, has been included – the 10th (2003), 12th (2007), and 17th (2017) editions. In addition, I referred to personal journals, letters, correspondence with many of the people who appear in these pages, and other research to write this book.

ACKNOWLEDGEMENTS

Thank you to the publishers and editors of the following magazines, newspapers, literary journals, and books where the following poems and essays (often in earlier versions) have previously appeared:

The Toronto Star: 2008, "Riding a train to Anywhere", appears in this book as "The Train to Anywhere"

The New Quarterly: 2008, "English Lesson 1: Greetings" and "English Lesson 3: The Interrogative" appear in this book as "The English School"

Somebody's Child, Touchwood Editions: 2011, "A Familiar Face"

Canadian Stories: 2009, "Entering the Cavern"

PRECIPICe: 2008, "Get Up and Spin"

Grain Magazine: 2010, "Shanti, Shanti", appears in this book as "The Travel Agent"

The Sun Magazine: 2009, "The Monk, the Woodcarver, and the Sage", appears in this book as "The Monk" and "The Woodcarver" and "The Sage"

The Nashwaak Review: 2009, "This is India", appears in this book as "The Boy on the Road"

Other Voices: 2008, "Waiting to Steal the Gods", appears in this book as "The Orphan"

The Best Women's Travel Writing. Volume 10: 2014, and *Traveler's Tales:* 2014, "Good is Coming", appears in this book as "The Sage"

The Nashwaak Review: 2009, "Reading the Flow", appears in this book as "Mother Ganges"

Forcefield: 77 Women Poets of British Columbia, Mother Tongue Publishers: 2013, and EVENT Magazine: 2009, "Varanasi Drafts", appears in this book as "The City of Light"

Kyoto Journal: 2013, "Heroes of the Hills", appears in this book at "The Acupuncturists"

S.i.W.C. Anthology: 2008, "Droplets of Hope", appears in this book as "The Doctor"

PRECIPICe: 2010, "Love in the Time of Silence", appears in this book as "The Volunteer"

Tower Poetry Society: 2008, "Between the Planks"

Room: 2009, "The Princess and the Poet"

The Globe and Mail: 2008, "Sights Unseen"

Conspicuous Accents: Accenti Magazine's Finest Stories of the First 10 Years, Longbridge Books: 2014, *Italian Canadians at Table: A Narrative Feast in Five Courses,* Guernica Editions: 2013, and *Accenti Magazine:* 2010, "This is Sunday Lunch"

The Globe and Mail: 2008, "Our Expiration Date"

The Globe and Mail: 2008, "Loneliness and Longing for Risotto"

Room: 2010, "Nabob Tins and Turkish Carpets"

The Globe and Mail: 2008, "Happy not to be a Mother", appears in this book as "St. Mary's Spring"

The Globe and Mail: 2011, "Driving– and Living– in the Slow Lane", appears in this book as "The Slow Lane"

Thank you to Libros Libertad publisher Manolis Aligizakis for his permission to use versions of several poems extracted from my 2010 poetry collection *Observations from Off the Grid*.

~

THESE STORIES BEGAN a decade ago in a studio apartment in Vigevano, Italy, where a boyfriend with a charming accent said, "Your new job is to write." Every day, as he taught music throughout the region of Lombardia, I sat down at a kitchen table facing a fourteenth-century brick wall and wrote. The stories continued – in an off-the-grid cabin on Haida Gwaii, a Craigslist sublet in Lake Cowichan, a snow-covered bungalow in Hokkaido, a renovated shed in my parents' backyard. And now I sit in Toronto's Pape Village, listening to police sirens and the rain.

Who to thank for all this? I could begin with the journalist from Lisbon whom I met while travelling in Morocco at the tender age of nineteen. "You have fire in your eyes," he said as we sat on a hotel rooftop looking out at the Sahara Desert. "You are meant to write." Never underestimate the power of such words on an insecure, fledgling writer. So, thank you, Tiago Franco.

Thank you to all the teachers, friends, lovers, and strangers who always seem to say the right thing at the right time. I hope you know my address book (yes, I still have one of those) is my greatest treasure. Many thanks to those who employ, house, and befriend transients.

Much gratitude to the writer-friendly *Radiant Press* for choosing me as one of their first authors, and to editor dee Hobsbawn-Smith for encouraging "Angie" to take ownership of her words.

Thank you to my parents who always answer their phone, and seem genuinely happy to hear my voice.

Thank you to the people of India who brought me back to life.

Finally, thank you to Giuseppe, who eventually left the jungles of Thailand to marry me, fulfilling both my secret wish to Amma and the prediction of a Varanasi fortune-teller.

ANGELA LONG IS A JOURNALIST and a poet. She has contributed to an extensive list of anthologies and periodicals, and has had articles published in The Globe and Mail and other newspapers. She is the author of a book of poetry, *Observations from Off the Grid* published in 2010, and has earned a BFA in Creative Writing from UBC as well as a Masters of Journalism from Ryerson. Currently Angela resides in Toronto, Ontario.